Successful Church Libraries

Successful Church Libraries

Elmer L. Towns

and

Cyril J. Barber

BAKER BOOK HOUSE ● Grand Rapids, Michigan

Standard Book Number: 8010-8768-6

Library of Congress Catalog Card Number: 75-1529-02

Copyright © 1971 by Baker Book House Company

Printed in the United States of America

Preface

The church today faces the alternative of advancing to meet the problems of the 70s or regressing into the past. Christian young people are demanding up-to-date answers to up-to-date problems. The church is being squeezed by cultural pressures and bombarded by the knowledge explosion.

Some churches are ignoring today's problems and are thrusting their spiritual heads into their own church ghettoes. Others are on the cutting edge of today's world and see God at work in their churches.

The church library, we believe, can play a significant part in revitalizing a church to meet today's challenges. But what is the condition of the church library? The average minister shakes his head and replies, "The church library is in sad shape," . . . if indeed he has a church library at all!

This book is designed to help the church that has no library but wishes to get one started, as well as to encourage the struggling church library.

Hopefully this book also will give a new direction to church libraries, for we believe that one of the primary goals of a church library should be that of strengthening the Christian education program of the church. It assumes that a church library is more than a depository of books from which church members occasionally check out certain titles — something more than a pleasant but unnecessary part of the church.

To be genuinely effective in assisting the church in its mission, the church library must be an educational resource center to which teachers and other church leaders look for assistance. Visual aids, audio-visual equipment, and reference sources then become an important part of the church library. Just as the quality of a college is measured by its library, so the quality of the educational program of the church may be gauged by its library.

Contents

Preface 5

1. The Library Committee 9
2. Appointing a Librarian 13
3. The Library Quarters 19
4. Financing the Library 22
5. Rules for the Library 29
6. Promoting the Library 32
7. Selecting Books and Equipment:
   General Guidelines 37
8. Book Selection: Suggestions for
   Acquiring a Basic Collection 42
9. Book Selection: One Hundred Paperbacks for
   Your Church Library 51
10. Preparation of Materials 58
11. The Circulation of Materials 77
12. An Introduction to the Dewey Decimal
    Classification System 86
13. Dewey Subject Guide for Easy Classification . . 93

Bibliography 99
Directory of Publishers 100
Directory of Library Supply and
Equipment Companies 103

1. The Library Committee

The first step in organizing a church library ought to be the appointment by the Board of Christian Education or the church board of a committee to organize and direct library affairs. The four or five members of this committee should represent all activities and age groups within the congregation (Sunday school, youth work, women's missionary group, camp, club work, etc.). This spread of representation will help the library to meet the needs of various groups for source material. An added benefit will be that news of the availability of materials will be carried back to these groups by their representative on the library committee.

Those appointed should have the following qualifications:

1. *The ability to discern, recognize and even seek out the resource materials* which are an important part of the modern church library. School teachers, those in publishing or merchandising, or those with artistic bents would probably be aware of the trends in Christian resource materials.

2. *Familiarity with or experience in library operation.* This prerequisite insures that the committee can become active without the need of training recruits. If people with this qualification are not available, someone on the committee should ask for help and advice from the local public or school librarian.

3. *An interest and desire to establish and promote a church library.* A person who is aggressive in upgrading

the church's total Christian education endeavor ought to be invited to serve on the library committee, for he will be more aware of its full potential to aid in communicating the Christian faith through up-to-date methods and materials and through a librarian who will energetically teach and encourage their use.

Those people who finally do constitute the library committee should understand their duties. These are:

1. *To appoint a librarian with the qualifications listed in Chapter 2.*

2. *To establish policies of and give direction to the library.* It must strive to meet effectively the best standards of Christian education and also serve the needs of individual church members.

3. *To provide the vision and motivation.* The committee will have no trouble fulfilling this duty in a church which is located in an educationally sophisticated community. However, the speed with which goals are met and the methods used in starting or upgrading the church library will always depend upon the church's geographic location, the available funds, and the spiritual, cultural and intellectual levels of the members of the church. This is not to say that a church in a poorer community ought to budget a lesser percentage for its library than does an affluent church. Churches in poorer communities actually have greater educational needs. Such a church should probably spend much more money on educational materials, with the special needs of its people as prime criteria for selecting these materials. The spiritual indoctrination of the unchurched or underprivileged child or adult must begin on a much simpler level than for those who at least know the language of the church. The new junior boy in a suburban Sunday school class interrupted the teacher to ask, "What is 'sin'?" At the other extreme of spiritual awareness, a sixth grader in the same Sunday school candidly inquired of his teacher during a lesson, "Is everyone

who died before Christ was born now in hell?" Such remarks indicate the wide range of needs with which the Sunday school teacher is confronted. The library committee is indirectly responsible for meeting this range of needs by providing teachers with the proper resource materials.

4. *To correlate library services with other agencies in the church.* This includes alerting department superintendents, teachers and group leaders to the supplementary materials which the library has purchased or plans to buy for various segments of the membership. They should then create opportunities for the librarian to demonstrate these new acquisitions. Library committee members should constantly alert themselves to the needs of groups within the church, then seek ways in which the library can help those groups accomplish their purposes. Committee members can also be active in demonstrating methods and materials. For example, one enthusiastic committee member realized that a tape recorder would be useful everywhere from the preschool to the home department of the Sunday school. The library purchased a moderately priced, easily operated model. The adult class teacher used it first — he taped his Sunday morning lesson to send to shut-ins of the church. This taping idea soon caught on. Pre-school teachers taped songs from phonograph records as an aid in class teaching of songs. Another teacher taped her class as they practiced for a special program; thus pupils were able to detect their own mistakes. Teen-agers who were using skits to become aware of real life situations in class taped these skits for self-criticism and appraisal of spiritual applications. This church soon found that one tape recorder was not sufficient for its use and the library committee purchased a second machine.

5. *To assume responsibility for selecting books, as well as educational equipment and materials.* (See Chapters 7 and 8.)

6. *To oversee the operation of the library.* The librarian cannot singlehandedly carry all the responsibility for enforcing rules, managing finances and supervising the performance of the library personnel. The committee must give assistance in this ministry. It is physically and emotionally impossible for one person to enforce every library rule and still fulfill the job of being a competent, helpful librarian. Others on the committee can set the example of acceptable library conduct and then instruct children, teen-agers and others in the correct use of the church library. Leaders and teachers will be borrowing and returning teaching aids both before and after almost any activity. Committee members should both encourage good library conduct and help to keep the flow of teaching materials operating smoothly.

The library must have efficient help to maintain its strength as the hub of the church educational program. The librarian himself should make clear (probably in writing) just what he expects of his helpers. The committee should also be discreetly aware of library assistants who are not performing well and who may be taking the librarian away from more important duties. If the removal of unsatisfactory help becomes necessary, the committee might work with the Board of Christian Education to first discover another type of job in the church for that person. Make him feel more needed in another place and he will probably be relieved to give up the library job. The committee needs patience in forming a competent, congenial team of workers.

7. *To act as a sounding board.* The librarian should be able to turn to the library committee for advice on new programs and projects which he or other church members propose as an extension of the church's ministry, including such matters as fund raising, promotion and any matters which are not specifically written into library policy.

2. Appointing a Librarian

The person chosen as church librarian will be the key to whether or not the library ultimately enhances the total ministry of the church; for, as in every other department of the church, no library will succeed without an enthusiastic, capable administrator. Nominating elderly or single persons as candidates for librarian simply because they have no other duties in the Sunday school or church is an illogical move. Any preconceived idea that a librarian must of necessity be stodgy and stuffy is equally absurd. If being elderly, or single, or unoccupied, is the committee's lone consideration for a librarian, top performance cannot be expected of the person chosen. Neither should possession of fine Christian character or a deep appreciation for books be the sole criteria for choosing a person for your church librarian. The person you choose may have some or all of these traits — none would necessarily detract — yet by themselves they do not qualify a person for the job at hand.

Survey your congregation for someone who meets the following criteria:

1. *Christian character.* The pastor or church officer who displays anything less than the highest spiritual character becomes suspect. The library committee, too, must appoint a man (or woman) whose life shows that Christ has redeemed him. He may be serving some who attend church but who have never met the Lord, as well as new and even unstable Christians.

2. *Cooperative spirit.* Some might say a cooperative

spirit is part of Christian character, and ideally it is. But not all persons of fine Christian character have the ability to work closely and well with other people. Some do their best work alone, without giving help or receiving it. The "loner" should probably not be asked to be church librarian, for the position has built into it constant interruptions and requests for help. The librarian must be open to new ideas from church leaders, members, friends, and even little children, since the library will serve them all. Those who are charged with the appointment of a librarian are probably already aware of the men and women in the congregation who seem to have no trouble getting along with others. Shouldn't they be placed on the "prospect" list for librarian to determine if they measure up in other ways? The untried person who holds no other job in the church should also be considered.

The librarian works under the supervision of the church board and the Board of Christian Education. Therefore, he must be subject to them and carry out their directions.

3. *An appreciation for books.* This qualification has a twofold meaning. The most helpful kind of librarian loves books for what they can give him personally, but he is also knowledgeable about all kinds of books for all types of people. Stand at the counter of your own public library some day and listen to a conversation between the librarian and those checking out books. The librarian has himself read many of the books, or at least reviews of them, and thus converses intelligently with borrowers about their reading material. This eavesdropping proves twice as interesting in the children's section. An interested librarian could tell a child the entire tale in the book the child has just selected, but he never does that. He tells just enough of the story to send the eager child scurrying home, anticipating the wonderful secrets awaiting him inside the covers.

The librarian should know how to infect people with the fever to read anything and everything good. He realizes that the church library should be equipped to meet the needs of everyone, from its scholars and teachers to the youngest and newest readers in the Sunday school.

4. *Organizational ability.* The librarian must keep his inventory neat and attractive, well supplemented and cataloged. He is responsible for maintaining regular library hours, whether or not he himself can be there. He chooses dependable helpers.

5. *Patience and persistence.* Some church members will besiege the library with requests for books both new and old. Others will be thankful if the librarian is not the type to tackle them and tie a book to them — the thought of reading carries absolutely no pleasure for them. But a patient, kind person behind the library desk can get to the most hardened nonreader. One church librarian was an intimate friend of a young mother who carefully avoided books. Her husband and children read avidly and she felt their discussion of magazine articles and books gave her sufficient stimulation. The librarian began pointing her friend to Christian books and magazines containing tips on child care and devotional helps, but at first the young mother felt no inner compulsion to read. She may have even been missing the blessing of reading God's Word. Then God allowed a serious physical problem to affect the family. The young mother turned to her librarian friend for Christian books which might help her understand why God sends sickness to families which have committed themselves to Him.

One little boy read nothing except by force, including, of course, his school books. A kindly church librarian took the time to show him the Christian adventure stories written just for his age. He began reading a book simply because the librarian had started telling him the story and he had to find out how it ended. He too became infected with this marvelous fever to live through the characters found in books.

A librarian cannot be expected to be able to retell every book, but he can enhance the church ministry by matching books to those who would most appreciate their content.

6. *Initiative and leadership ability.* Some may view the church library as a one-man operation which can be safely staffed by an introverted bookworm. He may be so efficient as to have computer-like knowledge of every book and who checked it out. He may in reality wish that each and every book stood safely in its appointed place on the library shelf. The library needs a broader and more open personality overseeing its operation.

The librarian's initiative will be evident when he introduces new ideas and trends to the attention of church officers. His leadership will show as he implements these ideas for the good of the congregation.

Skills of the Librarian

1. *Knowledge and/or experience in library work.* The person who has little knowledge of library mechanics, but who does have the time and interest, may quickly compensate by reading or by observing others who do have library skills. The committee may need to give an untried person the chance, if that person meets other requirements. The person who shows efficiency in other aspects of life would probably also be able to run the church library efficiently. This book is designed to help your appointee know where to go for organization help. Your public librarian might also be willing to aid the church in training a person for that office.

2. *Typing ability.* Lack of typing ability can be a real hindrance to the librarian, but he can compensate by enlisting some clerical help. This might be the place to try out church members who have no other jobs. If they fit in well on this comparatively simple assignment, they could be considered for other jobs.

Duties of the Librarian

The committee should not finalize its choice of a librarian until it has submitted a list of duties to the prospect. The person considering the position must decide whether he is willing and able to perform those duties. He should then meet with the committee, whose chairman should be prepared to again review the tasks which are expected of the church librarian, in order to avoid misunderstanding about the job and its ramifications.

Following is a list of duties of the librarian. The local church library committee will probably want to add to this list.

1. *Lead in selecting appropriate books and materials.* Particularly good sources from which to make selection of books are the catalogs and publication announcements of Christian publishers. Ask that the name of your church be placed on their mailing lists, read their notices yourself and pass them on to the leaders of clubs and other groups in the church to elicit suggestions for possible selection of new materials. Subscribe to Christian education magazines and display them for teacher use. Read reviews of new books from as many periodicals as possible; this will help you choose the best books for your library. Read or skim books which you think the library needs; know something of their content so that you can answer future inquiries by members. Note books which members request that you buy and try to fit them into your budget.

2. *Supervise the processing and shelving of books.*

3. *Maintain definite library hours* to coincide with the educational programs of the church. This means scheduling your assistants so that a knowledgeable clerk is always on hand to check out books and teaching resources.

4. *Supervise the checking out and returning of materials, and issue overdue notices.* Inefficiency in these operations will cause a breakdown of the library ministry. Strive to have this operation so firmly in hand that by

checking the records you can quickly ascertain whether or not a certain book is on the shelf. There is no guesswork in the efficient library. The records show who has checked out any book. Always offer to reserve it when it is returned. A church librarian is involved in God's ministry, and this fact should challenge him to be exceptionally conscientious in his work.

5. *Give courteous aid.* Often library patrons need help in locating books, equipment and materials.

6. *Maintain financial records.* Accurate records should be kept of both money received (as gifts, from overdue book fees, from the budget, and from book sales in the church) and funds dispersed for all library expenses. The librarian must also write a proposed budget and submit it to his committee for approval. Categories to be included in the budget are:

    a. Books.
    b. Visual aids.
    c. Visual aid equipment (screens, projectors, flannelgraphs, etc.). (These are costly items, so plan accordingly.)
    d. New library equipment (shelves, filing cabinets, etc.).
    e. Office and library supplies (stationery, typewriter ribbons, records, etc.).

7. *Attend Christian education conferences with the Sunday school staff.* Such conferences are excellent sources of information on new equipment and materials, as well as on new educational trends. Be present at all teachers' meetings of the local church, and be prepared to demonstrate the use of teaching aids or to review a new book that will be of genuine value to teachers.

8. *Take charge of promotion.* The librarian should write library items for local newspapers and the church bulletin, describing library services or new material and equipment.

3. The Library Quarters

The larger, well-supported church will be able to create a beautiful library with an educational atmosphere. The smaller church may have to "make do" and be satisfied with an environment that is less conducive to learning. However, money is not the final factor that determines the effectiveness of a church library. Imagination and initiative play a great part in providing an attractive and lively looking home for the church library.

If the church library is to be an educational resource center that serves the entire church, the library will house all books, materials and equipment used by group leaders and Sunday school teachers. Space provisions for adequate shelving and storage of the following must be made:

Reference Materials
    Bibles
    Bible college catalogs
    Commentaries
    Concordances
    Dictionaries
    Encyclopedias
    Maps and atlases
    Samples of Sunday school quarterlies

General Reading Materials
    Books
    Magazines

Audio-Visual Materials
    Film strips
    Flannel backgrounds and story sets
    Illustrated Bible verses

Movie projector(s)
Movie screen(s)
Overhead projector(s)
Phonograph(s)
Phonograph records, cataloged
Slide projector(s)
Split 35mm film projector(s)
Tape recorder(s) and cartridges
Teaching pictures

Service Materials
Absentee postcards (on display)
Birthday and welcome buttons
Extra take-home papers
Games
Musical instruments
Sheet music, cataloged
Supply catalogs

Audio-visual equipment is most efficiently stored in a separate closet which has been specially outfitted with shelves and cubbyholes for each item. The door of the closet could be used as a bulletin board.

If the audio-visual equipment cannot be stored in a separate room away from general view, it should be placed in such a way that the room does not appear cluttered. Perhaps the equipment can be shielded with decorative dividers or screens.

Adequate lighting always adds to the attractiveness of a room. If necessary, use table lamps to light up dark areas. Good lighting should also be found in the closets where equipment is stored.

Bright coats of paint also add to the pleasantness of a room. Rooms in an old church basement will often lose their dingy appearance by the application of cheery colored paint and the addition of more light.

Books show up better on shelves of a light color since many bindings come in dark shades. If the budget allows, carpet the floor for warmth and noise control.

Sufficient shelving, a desk and chair for the librarian, filing cabinets of both floor and tabletop size, and tables and chairs for patrons of the library are necessities. If the library room is too small to accommodate tables and chairs, perhaps they could be placed just outside the room.

Furnishings should be functional. Avoid overspending on expensive furnishings. A beautiful library with impressive furniture is useless if it is not matched by an equally impressive collection of books and equipment that is being used constantly. Both require the outlay of funds.

A librarian and his assistants can do much to give the library an inviting appearance. Decorative touches on bulletin boards and walls should be evident. If available, paintings or appropriate pictures will enhance the room. A few growing plants will add life to the library — but do not neglect them! Books should not be allowed to pile up; rather they should be reshelved each day. Files should be kept neat and orderly. Weed out old issues of magazines, pamphlets and catalogs.

4. Financing the Library

Many times the local church votes approval of a library and duly provides suitable quarters. A librarian is chosen, but somehow the project dies a slow death because the appointee receives nothing more than a couple of boxes of old books. The librarian may have the ingenuity to make good use of old books, and some benefit may accrue to the church, but much more is needed to develop a fine and adequate educational center within the church.

An illustration from one of those "old" books, better termed "Christian classics," exemplifies the use which God makes of the written word. Hudson Taylor, founder of the China Inland Mission in 1866, was used greatly by God. Mrs. Howard Taylor, his daughter-in-law, chronicled her father's spiritual and physical battles for the mission in the book, *Hudson Taylor's Spiritual Secret*. The opening chapters include this account from Taylor's childhood:

> The beginning of it all was a quiet hour among his father's books when young Hudson Taylor sought something to interest him.
>
> He took the story he found into a favorite corner of the old warehouse, thinking he would read as long as it did not get prosy. As the story did merge into something more serious, he was arrested by the words, "The Finished Work of Christ."
>
> One thought came with startling clearness, "If the whole debt is paid, what is there left for me to do?" The answer took possession of his soul, "There is nothing in the world for me to do save fall on my knees and accept this Saviour and His salvation, to praise Him forevermore."

God uses books, and that alone should be sufficient reason for churches to consider their library a sound financial investment. Capable new Christian writers appear in print year after year. They are perhaps the answer to our cry for relevance in the church.

The best kind of library financing follows church policies and assures a regular, dependable income. Evangelical church policy disallows most fund-raising methods. Ideally the church budget should include money to equip a new library or to increase the inventory and equipment of the already existing one. A Canadian church reported that enthusiasm for its library began to mount after members voted to support the library with 10 percent of the Sunday school offerings.

The following methods and suggestions have been effectively used to raise money for or to actually stock the church library.

1. *Class or group project.* Groups of individuals (e.g., Sunday school classes) within the church can often be challenged to help build a library inventory. The librarian can begin by supplying a list of needed books, including volumes for all ages and for varying ranges of interest. Books purchased as a class project will likely reflect the special interests of that class. For example, older adults might select devotional reading, novels, Bible study helps, and other reference books. The younger married and professional people would be interested in books about child care, marital problems and general psychology from the Christian point of view. There might be a theology or philosophy buff in the group, and he would surely vote for the work of his favorite author. The women's or youth class might provide funds for missionary adventures. The teens will prefer their favorite novelists and books written by prominent personalities such as athletes and beauty contest winners. Some will want to find Christian classics, and nearly every age group will sooner or later be look-

ing for program helps. Christian educators in the congregation will want to see the shelves stocked with books on teaching and student guidance. Fiction or biography catches the interest of most youngsters from junior high school age down, so that a teacher or department superintendent could challenge his girls and boys to give toward the purchase of some of their favorite story books. Teachers might contribute one of the numerous versions of Scripture, and thus make it available for supplementary use in class, along with the atlases and books of art, geology and geography. The list is as long and varied as are the fields of interest encompassed by the congregation.

2. *Library Sunday.* Such a special day might be incorporated as an annual event on the church calendar. The librarian could enlist the help of members in setting up special features for each service on that day. For example, a department superintendent could be prepared to tell the pictorial story (history) of the English Bible. (Written material, pictures and filmstrips may be obtained at low cost from the nearest chapter of the American Bible Society. For information write American Bible Society, 1865 Broadway, New York, N.Y. 10023.) Sunday school teachers could supplement their lessons with examples from books in the library, or from books on the "wanted list." He could then encourage the class to help buy books on "Library Sunday" through their gift in the special offering.

Here the "wanted list" comes into focus. In preparation for Library Sunday, the day the church asks for special money gifts for books, each member should already have been given a mimeographed list of books which the library needs, including prices. People could check off the book they wish to purchase, and make the appropriate donation. Knowing exactly what their money will buy will elicit greater donations from donors on this special day.

On Library Sunday the librarian or other capable person could be allotted time in the service to review a new or otherwise significant Christian book, preferably one which the library does not already have. Book reviews are also valuable in motivating the congregation to read volumes which are already on the shelves.

3. *Book clubs.* The library could organize a club whose members buy books, read them and then donate the volume to the church library. This need not be the type of high pressure group which the word *club* connotes. The advantage for members might simply be that they would obtain books from a publisher or bookstore at a discount. Many companies extend such discounts to churches, but rarely to individuals. This idea will appeal mainly to those who regularly buy and read books, including parents of children who read. Organization of such a club should fit the local situation, possibly being simply a list of people who wish to purchase books for the church at a discount.

4. *Memorial gifts.* Library publicity should occasionally indicate the fact that the church is prepared to accept books given in memory of loved ones, to mark the death of a special person (in the denomination or community), or to commemorate such events as church anniversaries, a pastor's years in Christian service, etc.

Donations to the library fund at the death of a loved one in the family must be acknowledged immediately with a special letter of condolence to the family. Gifts of books or donations for books given in lieu of flowers must be acknowledged to the donor, and the bereaved family should be notified, in writing within twenty-four hours after the arrival of the gift, that the donor chose this kind of condolence.

5. *Book showers.* Such a project might be sponsored by either the whole church or by an adult class or department of the Sunday school. A local Christian bookstore

would probably be willing to consign a shipment of books which have been selected jointly by the church and store manager. Many folks will not take the time to browse through a bookstore, but if a book table is arranged in conjunction with a church meeting, then such browsing turns out to be a pleasant experience. It can also be profitable for the library — for a book shower is meant to make books available for families to purchase as gifts to the library. Each purchaser is given first chance to check out the book he buys. The book shower gives special impetus to building the library inventory because people will far more quickly buy a book which they hold in their hand than one they must choose from a book list.

One church used a gift plan by designating the month of November as "Thanks Giving Month for the Library." The church ordered a consignment of books from a Christian bookseller with the option to return for full credit all unsold books. The advantage of this system is that the librarian has already selected desirable books, yet members can choose those which most interest them.

The theme of the month-long display was "Be Thankful for Written Words." Posters encouraged members to be actively thankful by giving a book to the library. "Progress posters" listed books which had been purchased for the library and their donors. All the books purchased were put on display so that people could become familiar with the new additions and plan to read them after they had been processed. A nameplate in each book designated its donor, and everyone who bought a gift book later received a written thank you from the library committee.

Expenses for this particular book shower came to $20, paid from the library budget; however, $300 worth of books were added to the library.

6. *A bookstore within the church.* A consignment of books stays in the church only temporarily — for Library Sunday, or for the duration of a Sunday school workers'

or missionary conference. However, some churches have felt that the advantages of having their own book-selling corner have far outweighed the arguments against such a venture. Some people feel strongly that no selling should be permitted in the church at any time. But some churches have stocked a book nook and opened it on the Lord's Day, and members are fully convinced that it is a ministry — an effective ministry.

The church wishing to open a book nook might do so in conjunction with its own library, and probably under the librarian's management. However, operating a book nook in conjunction with the church's own library collection presents the obvious problem of keeping separate the books for sale and those for lending.

Churches which have installed book nooks report encouraging results. Some congregations simply make their own selection of one or two hundred books, buy them from publishers (or take books on consignment from a Christian bookstore), and assign the profits to the church treasury. Other churches request that a bookstore consign a selection of books to the church for sale on the premises, and all money collected goes back to the bookstore. In both of these business arrangements the motive is to provide good literature for the use of the church members, certainly not to provide a further source of income for the church.

Churches that sell books have reported an interesting trend or two. Junior-age children purchase pocket books of good fiction. Were not these books so available, they would probably spend the money elsewhere, and possibly on something less profitable to themselves. Sunday school teachers scan the book nook for teaching aids, and they buy books as gifts for their class members.

7. *Want list.* The librarian should prepare a list of books (twelve to twenty-four) from which persons may select and purchase books as gifts to the library. He will

need to revise this list regularly, deleting acquired books and adding newly published ones. The librarian should also supplement this "wanted list" with another comprehensive listing of the titles and types of books which the church library will accept. With this list as a basis, the librarian can kindly but firmly refuse to shelve donations of books which do not enhance the library's purpose of communicating the Christian faith to people.

5. Rules for the Library

To function as an effective educational arm of the church, the library must formulate some rules which will not only regulate procedures, but encourage library use. A list of the rules which has been adopted by the library committee should be printed in a "Guide to the Library." Mimeographing is usually sufficient for the average church. Following are guidelines for formulation of rules which will probably be needed:

1. *Hours.* The library should be open at regular, specified times. This factor, plus the attractiveness of the room, will determine the initial response given to the new facility. For example, Sunday school teachers are often encouraged to arrive from ten to thirty minutes before classtime to get the classroom in readiness and to greet the students. The clerk or librarian should be on hand during this time to check out materials.

After church services, two activities will take place in the library. Church members will browse for books and will need help in checking them out. Teachers will be returning materials and perhaps be searching for the items necessary for next week's lesson. The librarian may need to train extra clerks to serve during hours of heaviest traffic, since he himself may not be able to be present all the time the library is open. A church should experiment to find the best library hours for itself.

2. *Use of the library.* Rules for use should indicate who may use the library and when they may use it. The library committee must specify when persons are welcome to use reference sources and check out books. Should this

list include church members, community members, other pastors, or only those who actually attend the church? Certain benefits come from welcoming community people. The adult who comes seeking a certain bit of information might be attracted to the Gospel in numerous ways. School children may ask to use your library while writing a report or term paper. These are opportunities to minister; however, they should not prevent full utilization of library services by those engaged in the Christian education ministry of the church.

It may be necessary to exclude all but teachers before Sunday school, especially if space and help are limited. If such a rule is necessary, Sunday school teachers should encourage the use of the library by students at other times.

3. *Period of loans of books and equipment.* The standard length of a book loan is two weeks; those in current demand may be borrowed for seven days. The librarian maintains a list of those next in line for a book in great demand. Rules for other procedures will have to be established: May a book be renewed? For how long and how many times? May someone (such as a shut-in) borrow or renew a book by telephone? What procedure should be followed in the event a book is returned in poor condition — with missing pages, perhaps, or otherwise marred?

The rules for loaning teaching aids must differ from those of books since the requests for these aids will be frequent. The librarian might post "sign-up" sheets for each piece of equipment, on which the teacher is asked to sign his name and the date he wishes to use the equipment. Through the sign-up sheet, other staff members will immediately be able to see whether or not a certain machine is available. The same method might be used to distribute seasonal teaching aids, thus eliminating the need for the librarian to search through her records for this information. When the budget allows, the librarian should plan to duplicate equipment which is in constant demand. Although usage should be encouraged, teachers should be discouraged from monopolizing teaching aids.

4. *Overdue fees.* Should there be a charge for overdue books, and if so, at what rate? Individual circumstances may indicate that no charges should be levied. However, a general policy of charging 2¢ for each day a book is past due (or 10¢ a week), would increase respect for library rules. Publicize the fact that overdue book fees go toward replacing books.

Exceptions to the past due rule may be made in cases of illness, for shut-ins, and cases where the librarian knows that a book has a special kind of ministry, such as the Sunday school teacher who keeps a book through a quarter to supplement his lesson preparation, or the person whose personal spiritual battle is being aided through a particular book.

5. *Books which have been lost or ruined.* If the family responsible for losing or ruining a book does not offer to replace it, the librarian must decide whether or not to buy another copy. Prior circulation of the book will help him determine this. Possibly it could better be replaced by a new publication. Repeated requests for a volume no longer in the library due to loss or damage would indicate that a new copy should be ordered.

The few remaining rules affect the mechanical operation of the library. The committee may need to consult a professional librarian, or at least a comprehensive handbook on library operation.

6. *Promoting the Library*

Any worthwhile Christian endeavor creates, and then maintains, a demand for its existence. The church library is no exception. The librarian and his committee must build the use of this educational facility so that the library becomes an indispensable part of the local ministry. Methods of promoting available services are only as wide as are the imaginations of those administering the library. In other words, the methods are endless. If the church can interest an aggressively artistic member in serving on the library committee, it may be guaranteeing acceleration of promotional activity. Even a relatively inexperienced teen who is showing artistic promise through the beginning courses at school might contribute to library promotion, under the direction, of course, of the librarian, who should always lead in promotional policy. Following are a number of suggestions to initiate and maintain interest in the library:

1. *Make the opening of a new church library an occasion for special attention.* A dedication service involving both library personnel and the Sunday school staff will draw attention to the library. Such a service, of course, is most appropriate after the library is furnished and equipped with a basic core of books. A dedication service provides a definite goal toward which work might be more speedily completed.

2. *A library open house* might be arranged, complete with refreshments. Give visitors an opportunity to view the newest books, teaching aids and equipment. The em-

phasis should be for everyone (not just Christian education leaders) to "come and see," rather than to "check
it out for use right now" — at least not until the official
hours for open house are past. People could use "sign-up"
lists to reserve their choices of books and equipment.

After the library has been inaugurated, teachers and
superintendents should arrange to meet with their students for one class session in the library, at which time the
librarian can acquaint the different age groups with the
kinds of services offered to them.

During the next teachers' meeting the librarian could
present a talk on the audio-visual resources of the library.
Materials and equipment should be displayed and demonstrated. The librarian should specifically point out to
new teachers the items available for the age groups they
are teaching. For such a conference the librarian might se-
cure from the Sunday school supplier enough catalogs so
that each staff member may keep one for future reference. Christian publishers are often quite willing to coop-
erate in this manner.

On the Sunday of an all-church open house for the library (especially for larger congregations), people could
be invited to attend in class groups at designated hours.
Such an arrangement is advantageous for the librarian,
because he is then able to emphasize different segments
of the library, explaining each more thoroughly.

3. *Make new posters at least each quarter.* Advertise
the library ministry by displaying posters in appropriate,
heavily-trafficked areas of the building. Feature seasonal
trends, such as winter, when people are generally more
confined and may have more time to read.

The junior department of the Sunday school may enjoy
a poster-making contest to advertise the ministry of the
library. An appropriate book could be awarded as first
prize and the posters displayed throughout the church.
As the different mothers and fathers view the posters to

determine which is best, they will become "sold" on the ministry of the library in an indirect manner.

4. *Locate the library bulletin board strategically* — as near the main entrance of the church as possible, so that many people will see it. The bulletin board may be utilized to display posters or an arrangement of dust jackets from recently acquired books. The library staff should also regularly post a list of new books on the library bulletin board. News notes, clippings, book reviews, and other media should be used to catch the eye and encourage further reading. Try to add something new every week.

5. *Observe special days.* On certain days on the church calendar, a display of books can be arranged in the church foyer. The librarian might be present to encourage people to check out books and to discover what new books are available. People who are not likely to make their way to the library may check out a book and benefit from reading it. Most librarians would suggest that this exhibit be small. It may include some pamphlets or magazines. The display should tie in with the occasion being observed. For instance, books on missions should appear during the missionary conference, and books on Easter, Christmas, Thanksgiving or other holidays should highlight those special seasons. If the pastor is giving a series of sermons on a specific portion of the Bible, books relating to this topic could be put in the foyer and checked out by those who want to do further study.

6. *Book reviews* can and should be used in a number of ways for maximum effectiveness in promoting the library. Making your librarian the only person responsible for giving book reviews has two disadvantages. First of all, the membership gets acquainted with new books from just one person's point of view. Secondly, the librarian defeats his purpose of encouraging other people to enjoy books. Let others give book reviews. However, since every reader is not capable of giving oral or written book re-

ports, the librarian needs to be somewhat selective in designating this duty. There are a variety of ways in which book reviews may appropriately be used in the church. Here are a few suggestions:

a. Schedule five minutes in the church service for a review of a significant, newly acquired book. This would be particularly effective if it related to the preaching topic of that day.

b. Schedule five minutes in a department or class for the presentation of a new book for a special age group, or one which relates to present lesson material. Teachers have much latitude in choosing books for this purpose. Subjects of the books reviewed could range from Bible study to Christian novels.

c. Have someone who has been helped in some definite area of Christian living by a particular book he has read give a personal testimony.

d. Use book reviews occasionally as part of activities of all groups within the church: youth groups, women's missionary meetings, boys' and girls' clubs and weekend retreats.

7. *Book Clubs.* Due to the competitive nature of the activity, book clubs probably work best with children and young people. They can probably be used most successfully in the summer when most children are free from school pressures. In a book club, children work against a deadline to read the highest number of books. The child gets credit for a given book by giving an oral or written review to the librarian. At the end of the designated period, first, second and third prizes (books, of course!) are given to the three reading the largest number of books. A book club of this type assumes two things: that a church can supply the necessary books, and that they will be given credit only for Christian books. Caution: Re-

stricting books read to those from the church library will eliminate the use of Christian books given to children by their parents.

8. *Library skits.* These may be humorous or serious performances, including acting out a portion of a book. This device is best used in youth or women's meetings.

9. *Pre-session activity* of the Sunday school. Many children arrive at Sunday school early. To keep these children occupied until the Sunday school worship begins a story "hour" (10 to 15 minutes in length) might be organized. If there is no room in the library before Sunday school begins, perhaps a room adjacent to the library could be used for this meeting. Someone other than the librarian or teachers should be asked to regularly read or tell a story.

10. *General and topical book lists* can be distributed to the different groups, such as teachers, officers, leaders (especially those newly elected), new members, children, youth, newlyweds, and parents.

11. *A library column in the church newspaper.* Here book reviews may appear along with news of new books and materials.

12. *Promotional book jackets* might be used to cover hymnals and books loaned by the library. If well designed and in good taste, such jackets will be effective.

13. *Home ministry.* Send church library books to those who are sick or shut in. The pastor and others who do home calling have a built-in reason to enter a home if they come bearing a helpful book. It can also guarantee a reason for a return visit to pick up the book. Callers should find out something of the background and interests of the person for whom he is choosing reading material.

7. Selecting Books and Equipment

General Guidelines

The librarian and library committee have the final decision on library inventory, for they, after all, are responsible for the operation of the library and should be able to determine whether or not the library is attaining its goal of assisting in communicating the Christian faith.

Although numerous books have the potential of enhancing and enriching the lives of individual Christians, they must be excluded from a church library because they are not Christian in purpose. It is obvious too that thousands of books do have a specifically Christian purpose, but no church library is in a position to purchase all of them. Even if a church library had unlimited funds to purchase books, the need for many of the books could not be demonstrated.

Following are some general guidelines for adding to and "weeding" the collection of a church library.

1. *Is the book true to Biblical ideals and doctrines?* Not every so-called Christian theologian has remained within the Biblical confines of truth in formulating his theology. Writers other than Christians have written for the church, but these authors have no place in the church library. Only books that contribute to the goals of the church belong in the church library.

2. *Is the price of the book in balance with your library budget or would its purchase prohibit the purchase of other needed books?* Remember, however, that a high

priced book may also have high value for the congregation, in which case its purchase should be seriously considered. Such a volume might be found in a second-hand store; a lower priced book with comparable content might also be considered.

3. *Is the subject matter fairly discussed or is the author decidedly biased?* How well does the author express himself and support his opinions through reference to authorities on the subject?

4. *Is the material covered factual, accurate, reliable, authoritative and up-to-date?* Is it based on latest research on child care and family psychology or in the newest trend for the subject being covered? Although an author may have been contemporary for his time, culture changes every decade. Principles that were effective ten years ago may be outmoded today. Methods change. Although the message of the Bible does not change, the science of Bible interpretation continually unfolds new applications and facts about Scripture. The Bible must be applied anew to every generation. The reader wants to know that a book has been written by a man knowledgeable and respected in his field.

5. *Will the book appeal to the age or interest group for whom it is written?* Library shelves should not be crowded with obviously low circulation books. Choose those which will have immediate appeal to definite age and interest groups. For example, books of planned programs are always in demand by teens and church leaders.

6. *Is the style of the book attractive?* Is the vocabulary, sentence structure and format appropriate for the age to which it is directed? Most advertising copy meets high standards of publication; public schools demand textbooks of high quality both in content and format. Some Christian books, however, fall short of meeting high standards of form and style. Make sure the books chosen are up-to-date in content and format.

7. *Is the physical makeup of the book satisfactory?* This includes binding, paper, and print. Will the paper and binding hold up well under hard use? Is the print clear and easy to read? Paperback books were once considered inappropriate for libraries due to their short life expectancy. Today, however, many books are available only in paperback, and higher quality paper and better binding assure a longer life.

8. *Do the illustrations complement the text and give it increased instructional value?* Is the subject matter arranged logically? Is it clearly outlined and indexed so that a reader can find certain information without reading the entire book? Remember, readers tend to choose the more appropriately and attractively illustrated book. Christian books are notorious for out-of-date pictures.

9. *Have the author and publisher established good reputations for books in the field?* New publishing companies are encountered less often than new authors, of course. Have the author's qualifications been well-documented by his publisher? Have experts in the field recommended this book?

10. *Has the volume been included in recent book lists or has it been reviewed in contemporary periodicals?* Judgment of the caliber of a given book may be made by reading reviews of it. Whether its particular slant will meet the needs of a particular church library may also be discovered. For instance, a new Christian education title might spark a librarian's interest; from a review he will be able to discover whether the volume was written strictly as a college textbook or was directed at the local church teacher.

The same general guidelines for choosing books apply to choosing visual aid materials and equipment, with these additions:

1. *Purchase materials from companies with well-established reputations for high educational standards.*

2. *Buy equipment from dealers who are known for dependable service of the equipment they have sold.*

3. *Consider the cost.* Remember that more expensive pieces of equipment often pay for themselves by giving better and longer service than the cheaper models. Thus it is best to consider the amount of use the teaching aid will be put to by the church and buy the equipment which will best serve the purpose.

The committee will probably want to work from the following criteria in accepting or rejecting books, materials and equipment that may be donated to the library:

1. *A book must help fulfill the library's purpose by fitting into one of the previously outlined categories.* Complete book collections might not be appropriate. Permission should be secured from the donor to dispose of unneeded books by passing them on to the local public or college library or by selling them, with the proceeds earmarked for new books.

2. *A book must be in usable condition.* Books with broken backs and yellowed, brittle, or missing pages have no place on the church library shelf. Rebinding a book that would be a valuable addition to the library might be considered. Anyone offering an old and valuable but damaged book should be informed of the limited use of such a book and that the book might have to be withheld or be restricted to limited circulation to prevent further damage. At all costs the church library must be kept functional.

3. *Shelves must not be overbalanced with one type of book or with one title.* Should this happen, the committee should weed out its collection and sell the books to be disposed of to church members, the proceeds again going for new titles; or the books might be offered to another library. The usefulness of your library is decreased by

keeping unneeded books, since they occupy space needed for newer and more useful volumes.

4. *Determine whether the cost of repair exceeds the value of the donated equipment that is in need of repair.* The library budget should allow for repairs, but the total repair budget should not be spent on marginal-use items.

8. Book Selection

Suggestions for Acquiring a Basic Collection

The church library can become one of the most effective educational agencies in the entire church and can be the means of bringing blessing to a great number of people. However, conceiving an idea and executing it are two entirely different matters. You will need a plan of action, some guidelines on how to proceed, if you are to be successful.

Once you have decided to establish a library or upgrade an existing one, you are immediately faced with stocking the library with books — the very best books on the market, the ones that will bring the greatest enrichment and edification to the people who will read them. This chapter and the following one were written to assist you in acquiring good books. The many suggestions which they contain represent the best in evangelical literature on the market today.

All the books suggested in this chapter are available in hardbound editions. Some of them are also available in paperback editions (see Chapter 9). Consideration of the amount of use anticipated and the availability of funds will determine which edition will be the best choice for your library.

To facilitate ordering the books which are suggested, the publisher of each title is given in parentheses. A list of publishers and their addresses is included in the appendices of this book.

General Works

A good concordance is a must, and one of the best is the *Exhaustive Concordance to the Bible* by James Strong (Abingdon). Another is by Alexander Cruden. If you buy Cruden's Concordance, do *not* get an abridged edition! Your library should also have one or two Bible dictionaries and a Bible atlas. Two good one-volume Bible dictionaries are available today — *The New Bible Dictionary* edited by J. D. Douglas (Eerdmans) and *Unger's Bible Dictionary* (Moody) vie for supremacy. Douglas' work represents the best in British scholarship while Unger's is more consistent and more complete. Later on you will want to add a multivolume work, and you should give careful consideration to Zondervan's forthcoming *Pictorial Encyclopedia of the Bible* edited by Merrill C. Tenney. For a Bible atlas your first preference should be *Zondervan's Pictorial Bible Atlas* by E. M. Blaiklock. An atlas by two Jewish scholars, Johanan Aharoni and Michael Avi-Yonah, *Macmillan Bible Atlas,* represents the latest in liberal scholarship.

As far as studies on the whole Bible are concerned, it would be hard to get anything better than the *General Introduction to the Bible* by Norman L. Geisler and William E. Nix (Moody) and *Explore the Book* by J. S. Baxter (Zondervan). You should also include the timely *Unger's Bible Handbook* by Merrill F. Unger (Moody) and Gleason Archer's *Survey of Old Testament Introduction* (Moody). When studying the Bible we often overlook books which deal specifically with *how* to study the Bible. *Joy of Discovery* by Oletta Wald (Bible Banner Press), *Independent Bible Study* by Irving Jensen (Moody), *How to Search the Scriptures* by Lloyd Perry and Robert Culver (Baker) and *Effective Bible Study* by Howard Vos (Zondervan) should definitely be included in your early acquisitions. Later on you should also buy the series of books by Joseph M. Gettys on *How to Study* . . . and *How to Teach* . . . (John Knox).

In the field of Bible history, archaeology, manners and customs, and geography, you would do well to consider Alfred Edersheim's *Bible History: Old Testament,* two volumes (Eerdmans), *Ancient Orient and the Old Testament* by Kenneth Kitchen (Inter-Varsity), *Everyday Life in Bible Times* by the National Geographic Society, *Archaeology and the Old Testament* by Merrill F. Unger (Zondervan), *Archaeology and Bible History* by Joseph Free (Scripture Press), and *The Biblical World* by Charles F. Pfeiffer (Baker).

Accurate interpretation should be the aim of every teacher of the Word of God and *Protestant Biblical Interpretation* by Bernard Ramm (Baker) and *Principles of Expository Preaching* — a book dealing with interpretation in spite of its title — by Merrill F. Unger (Zondervan) should be high on your priority list.

Bible Helps

Many excellent commentaries are available in inexpensive paperbacks. This is true of *Everyman's Bible Commentary* (Moody) which contains some of the finest expository material we have found anywhere. These brief commentaries may be used as "handbooks" in home Bible classes.

Genesis: A Devotional Commentary by W. H. Griffith Thomas (Eerdmans) is excellent for a study of Genesis 12-50, and the two-volume work by H. C. Leupold, *Exposition of Genesis* (Baker) is invaluable. Alan Redpath has written two fine devotional books on Joshua and Nehemiah. They are *Victorious Christian Living* and *Victorious Christian Service* (Revell). *The Psalms* by W. Graham Scroggie (Revell) and *Exposition of the Psalms* by H. C. Leupold (Baker) should both be in your library. H. A. Ironside on *Daniel the Prophet* (Loizeaux), Robert Culver's *Daniel and the Latter Days* (Moody), and Edward Young's *Prophecy of Daniel* (Eerdmans) are also good books for your shelves. Other studies in the books of the Old Testament can be added as the Sunday School curriculum requires them.

Where the New Testament is concerned, the commentaries by Charles Erdman (Westminster) are excellent. They are now available in paperback and are quite inexpensive. Everett Harrison's *Introduction to the New Testament* (Eerdmans), W. Graham Scroggie's *Guide to the Gospels* (Revell), and G. Campbell Morgan's expositions (four volumes), *Studies in the Four Gospels* and *Acts of the Apostles* (Revell) are mandatory. For the rest, the writings of William Hendriksen on the *Gospel of John, Ephesians, Philippians, Colossians and Philemon, First and Second Thessalonians,* and *First and Second Timothy and Titus* (Baker) are all excellent. You will also want H. A. Ironside on *Romans* and *Corinthians One* and *Corinthians Two* (Loizeaux). Alan Cole has made a fine contribution to evangelical literature with his *Commentary on the Gospel According to Mark* and *Commentary on the Epistle of Paul to the Galatians* (Eerdmans), and no library is complete without F. F. Bruce's *Commentary on the Acts of the Apostles* (English text edition) and *Commentary on the Epistle to the Hebrews* (Eerdmans). Francis Foulkes' *Commentary on the Epistle of Paul to the Ephesians,* Alan Stibbs' *Commentary on First Epistle of Peter,* Michael Green on *Second Peter and Jude,* and John Stott's *Commentary on the Johannine Epistles* (Eerdmans) are all good.

Bible Doctrine

In the general area of Bible doctrine you should have Chafer's *Major Bible Themes* (Zondervan), William Evans' *Great Doctrines of the Bible* (Moody), *Baker's Dictionary of Theology* edited by Everett F. Harrison (Baker), and

L. Berkhof's *Summary of Christian Doctrine* (Eerdmans). Then, in the area of the inspiration and authority of the Scriptures, Edward Young's *Thy Word Is Truth* (Eerdmans) and Clark Pinnock's *Defense of Biblical Infallibility* (Presbyterian and Reformed) should be available to your readers. Charles Ryrie has an excellent handbook on *The Holy Spirit* (Moody) and to this may be added *The Holy Spirit of God* by W. H. Griffith Thomas (Eerdmans) and *The Person and Work of the Holy Spirit* (Moody) by René Pache. *Jesus Christ Our Lord* by John F. Walvoord (Moody), *Things to Come* by J. Dwight Pentecost (Zondervan), and *The Return of Jesus Christ* by René Pache (Moody) will give you some first rate works on different facets of Bible doctrine.

Devotional Books

There are many good inspirational books and the works of Andrew Murray, F. B. Meyer, Donald Grey Barnhouse, J. B. Phillips, and Ruth Paxson are considered standard. Some new books have been published recently and these deserve notice: *Balancing the Christian Life* by Charles Ryrie (Moody) and *Pattern for Maturity* by J. Dwight Pentecost (Moody) are excellent. Other timeless favorites are *The Christian's Secret of a Happy Life* by Hannah W. Smith (Revell), and *The Threefold Secret of the Holy Spirit* by James H. McConkey (Moody).

Apologetics

A well-rounded library will have a good selection of books on apologetics (the defense of Christianity). These should include two books by Henry M. Morris, *Twilight of Evolution* (Baker) and *Studies in the Bible and Science* (Baker), Bolton Davidheiser's *Evolution and the Christian Faith* (Baker), *Man's Origin, Man's Destiny* by A. E. Wilder Smith (Harold Shaw), Clark Pinnock's *Set Forth Your Case* (Presbyterian and Reformed), *The Gene-*

sis Flood by J. C. Whitcomb and H. M. Morris (Presbyterian and Reformed), Bernard Ramm's *Protestant Christian Evidences* (Moody), and a very popular book by
Paul Little, *Know Why You Believe* (Inter-Varsity).
In the area of Evangelism you need Paul Little's *How
to Give Away Your Faith* (Inter-Varsity) and W. D. Rob-
erts' *Revolution in Evangelism* (Moody).

Church History, Cults, Etc.

Earle Cairns' work *Christianity Through the Centuries*
(Zondervan) should be regarded as the basic work with
which to start. From here you can enlarge your library as
you sense a need for further material.
Walter Martin's booklets on *Jehovah's Witnesses, Mormonism, Herbert W. Armstrong,* and *The Kingdom of the
Cults* (Bethany Fellowship) should have a place in your
library with William Biederwolf's *Russellism Unveiled,
Mormonism Under the Searchlight, Seventh-day Adven-
tism,* and *Spiritualism* (Eerdmans).

Children's Books

No library should be without the *Sugar Creek Gang*
series by Paul Hutchens (Moody and Eerdmans), Bernard Palmer's *Danny Orlis* series (Moody), Paul White's
Jungle Doctor series (Eerdmans), and the other books in
the Moody Pre-teen and Moody Teen series.
In addition, you should have a children's Bible; Ken
Taylor's *Bible in Pictures for Little Eyes, Devotions for
the Children's Hour,* and *Stories for the Children's Hour*
(Moody) are excellent.

Biographies, Missionary Stories, Adult Books

Adults will require something a little more challenging
if they are to be spiritually enriched by what they read.
Lines of a Layman by J. C. Penney of the Penney Stores

(Eerdmans) and *Search for Reality* by Gary Collins (Key Publications) should prove stimulating reading. *Ascent to the Tribes* by Isobel Kuhn, *Behind the Ranges* by Mrs. Howard Taylor, *Mover of Men and Mountains*, the autobiography of Robert G. LeTourneau, *Splinters from an African Log* by Martha Wall (Moody), *The Bamboo Cross, Christ's Witchdoctor*, and *Out of the Jaws of the Lion* by Homer Dowdy (Harper and Row) are all excellent. To these may be added the books by Elizabeth Elliott, Bruce Porterfield, and the standard biographies about William Carey, Hudson Taylor, Adoniram Judson, David Brainerd, and the other great pioneers.

It is amazing how little Christians know of their heritage. Biographies of men who shaped Christianity would go a long way towards dispelling much of the inertia in our churches today. *Captive of the Word* about Martin Luther and *John Wesley: The Burning Heart* both by J. Skevington Wood (Eerdmans) and *Spurgeon, Heir of the Puritans* by Ernest W. Bacon (Eerdmans) should be read and re-read. J. C. Pollock has written about *Moody* (Macmillan) and so has James F. Findlay, Jr. His work, *Dwight L. Moody: American Evangelist*, is published by University of Chicago Press. Roland Bainton's *Here I Stand* on Luther (Abingdon) and *Erasmus of Christendom* (Scribner) are worthy additions to your shelves; and *The Man God Mastered*, a life of John Calvin, by Cadier (Eerdmans) should be there as well. Francis Asbury, George Whitfield, and other great reformers and revivalists should be given prominence, too. You can enlarge this section as time goes by.

Bible biographies have a perennial appeal to the people of God. They make the truth of God's Word relevant as readers find the application of the Word to their needs in the way others faced similar trials and temptations, problems and perplexities, sorrows and successes. Excellent books in this category are *Robust in Faith* by J. Oswald

Sanders (Moody). *Light of the Cross* by Stuart Barton
Babbage (Zondervan), and works on individual characters like *John the Baptist* and *Life Through the Cross* by
Marcus Loane (Zondervan), *David, A Man After the
Heart of God* and *Elijah, A Man of Like Nature* by Theodore Epp (Back to the Bible), *Studies in the Life of
Christ* (three volumes) by R. C. Foster (Baker), *The Story
of the Cross* by Leon Morris (Eerdmans), *A Short Life of
Christ* by Everett F. Harrison (Eerdmans), and *Apostle Ex-
traordinary* by Reginald White (Eerdmans), to name a
few.

Youth's Problems, Courtship, Marriage

With problems facing our youth it *often* remains for the
church to supply the answers which the home has failed
to provide. Drug addiction, promiscuity, and delinquency
can be effectively answered from the Christian's point of
view; and *Helping Youth Avoid Four Great Dangers* by
Hal and Jean Vermes (Association Press) should be read by
every parent. *The Great Sex Swindle* by John W. Drake-
ford (Broadman) and the writings of Evelyn Mills Duvall,
e.g. *Why Wait Till Marriage, Love and the Facts of Life,*
etc. (Association Press), available in paperback, should
be purchased for your library. Her *The Church Looks at
Family Life* (Broadman) is also worthwhile; and C. W.
Scudder's *Crises in Morality, Danger Ahead,* and *The Family in Christian Perspective* (Broadman) should be acquired as soon as your budget permits. From a positive
point of view, youth should be prepared for marriage and
here Dwight Small's *Design for Christian Marriage* (Revell), W. C. Field's *Unity in Marriage* (Concordia), and
This Way to Happiness by Clyde Narramore (Zondervan)
are indispensable. And for those who are married and
find that the communication gap seems to be widening,
Dwight H. Small's *After You've Said I Do* (Revell) is a
must!

Books for Church Members

Many people have no idea of what it is like to be a pastor and *Help Your Minister Do His Best* by Owen Weatherly (Judson) will give them greater understanding of what is required of him and how they can help him. Lloyd M. Perry's *Manual of Pastoral Problems and Procedures* (Baker) is a handy book. D. James Kennedy's *Evangelism Explosion, The Coral Ridge Program for Lay Witness* `(Tyndale House) and Charles Ryrie's *Place of Women in the Church* (Moody) are worthy of consideration. Other helpful books dealing with ushering, the church secretary and staff, and the ministry of stewardship are: W. O. Garrett's *Church Usher's Manual* (Revell), Katie L. Myers' *The Church Secretary* (Seabury), Herman J. Sweet's *Multiple Staff in the Local Church* (Westminster), William L. Howse's *Church Staff and Its Work* (Broadman) and George M. Bowman's *Here's How to Succeed with Your Money* (Moody).

Workers in the church will also appreciate having on hand Ethel Barrett's *Storytelling: It's Easy* (Zondervan), Findlay Edge's *Teaching for Results* and *Helping the Teacher* (Broadman), Lois Le Bar's *Focus on People in Church Education* (Moody), Herbert W. Byrne's *Christian Education in the Local Church* (Zondervan), Kendig B. Cully's *Westminster Dictionary of Christian Education* (Westminster), Kenneth O. Gangel's *Leadership for Church Education* (Moody), *Adult Education in the Church* by Roy Zuck and Gene A. Getz (Zondervan), and Jack Hyles' *Sunday School Manual* (Sword of the Lord Publishers) as well.

You will not be able to get all of these books all at once. However, you should plan to buy whatever you can within the limits of your budget and try to obtain the others by the means suggested in Chapter 4.

9. Book Selection

One Hundred Paperbacks for Your Church Library

Chapter 8 was devoted to the basic books which you will want to add to your library as soon as finances permit. They are all books of *quality* and will form the finest possible basis upon which to build your collection. Your purchasing power will be controlled by your budget and, because there are many necessary items which you will have to buy before you can effectively operate as a library (supplies such as book cards and pockets, date due slips, stamps, etc.), your early acquisitions will be limited. In an endeavor to help you get good *quantity* as well as quality we are suggesting that you begin with some well-chosen paperbacks. Paperbacks are relatively inexpensive and, while they will not last as long as clothbound books, they will help you get started much faster.

While paperbacks are emphasized in this chapter, do not overlook the basic essentials listed in Chapter 8.

Here are one hundred paperbacks we recommend:

Adair, James R., ed. *Unhooked.* Grand Rapids: Baker Book House, 1971. Dramatic stories of those who became addicted to drugs but came back.

Banks, William L. *Jonah: The Reluctant Prophet.* Chicago: Moody Press, 1966. A useful book for personal Bible study.

Barrett, Ethel. *Storytelling: It's Easy.* Grand Rapids: Zondervan Publishing House, 1960. *The* book on the subject.

Blaiklock, E. M. *Mark: The Man and His Message.* Chicago: Moody Press, 1967.

—————. *St. Luke: Scripture Union Bible Study Books.* London: Scripture Union, 1966. Available from Eerdmans. A good book in a good series.

Bockelman, Eleanor. *The Stewardess.* Minneapolis, Minn.: Augsburg Publishing House, 1956. A book for those who feel left out of "church work."

Bounds, E. M. *Purpose in Prayer.* Chicago: Moody Press, n.d. Excellent!

Bruce, Frederick Fyvie. *The New Testament Documents: Are They Reliable?* Grand Rapids: Wm. B. Eerdmans Publishing House, 1966. An affirmative answer defending the books in the New Testament.

Bye, Beryl. *Teaching our Children the Christian Faith.* Chicago: Moody Press, 1966. A book every parent should read . . . and then practice.

Clark, Gordon H. *Peter Speaks Today.* Philadelphia: Presbyterian and Reformed Publishing Company, 1967. An excellent devotional treatment of Peter's First Epistle.

Collins, Gary. *Search for Reality.* Wheaton: Key Publications, 1969. A timely, relevant treatment of psychology and Christianity from a strongly evangelical position.

Cook, Robert A. *Leveling with God.* Grand Rapids: Zondervan Publishing House, 1967.

—————. *It's Tough to be a Teenager.* Grand Rapids: Zondervan Publishing House, n.d. Two good books for those in their teens.

—————. *Now that I Believe.* Chicago: Moody Press, 1960. One of *the* best books to place in the hands of a new Christian!

Cramer, George H. *First and Second Peter.* Chicago: Moody Press, 1967. A worthy addition to the *Everyman's Bible Commentary* series.

Duvall, Evelyn Mills and Reuben Hill. *Being Married.* New York: Association Press, 1960.

—————. *When You Marry.* New York: Association Press, 1962. Two good books for those in their late teens or early twenties.

Edman, V. Raymond. *They Found the Secret.* Grand Rapids: Zondervan Publishing House, n.d. The spiritual experiences of twenty notable Christians.

Epp, Theodore. *Flesh and Spirit in Conflict.* Lincoln, Nebraska: Back to the Bible Broadcast, 1968. Practical studies in the letter to the Galatians.

—————. *Job: A Man Tried as Gold.* Lincoln, Nebraska: Back to the Bible Broadcast, 1967.

—————. *The Other Comforter.* Lincoln, Nebraska: Back to the

Bible Broadcast, 1967. Practical studies in the person and work of the Holy Spirit.

Erdman, Charles R. *Commentaries on the New Testament.* 17 Vols. Philadelphia: Westminster Press, 1919-1936. Choice expositions on the theme and purpose of every book in the New Testament.

Gettys, Joseph M. *How to Study First Corinthians.* Richmond, Va.: John Knox Press, 1960.

_____. *How to Teach First Corinthians.* Richmond, Va.: John Knox Press, 1956. Two excellent, helpful books. Part of a whole series on *how* to study and teach the Word of God.

Gillies, Donald. *Unity in the Dark.* London: Banner of Truth Trust, 1964. A thorough exposé of the ecumenical movement.

Green, Michael. *Man Alive.* Chicago: Inter-Varsity Press, n.d.

_____. *Runaway World.* Chicago: Inter-Varsity Press, n.d. Two clear-cut books vindicating the Christian faith and showing Christianity to be the only plausible answer to the futility and hopelessness facing people today.

Griffiths, M. *Consistent Christianity.* Chicago: Inter-Varsity Press, n.d.

_____. *Take My Life.* Chicago: Inter-Varsity Press, n.d. Two timely books dealing with *what* a Christian should do and *how* he should conduct his life.

Harrison, Norman B. *His Salvation.* Minneapolis, Minn.: The Harrison Service, Inc., n.d.

_____. *His Side Versus Our Side.* Minneapolis, Minn.: The Harrison Service, Inc., n.d. Two of Dr. Harrison's many books. Devotional, practical and edifying.

Hiebert, D. Edmond. *First Timothy.* Chicago: Moody Press, 1957.

_____. *Second Timothy.* Chicago: Moody Press, 1958. Two valuable books which, with the author's other work on *Titus,* aid immeasurably in the mastery of the pastoral epistles.

Houghton, Frank. *Faith's Unclaimed Inheritance.* London: Inter-Varsity Fellowship, 1964.

Houston, Jack. *Wandering Wheels.* Grand Rapids: Baker Book House, 1970. The story of young men who ride bicycles from coast to coast, all the time sharing their faith.

Jensen, Irving L. *Numbers: Journey to God's Rest-Land.* Chicago: Moody Press, 1968. A brief commentary by the author of *Independent Bible Study.*

Johnson, Douglas. *The Christian and His Bible.* Grand Rapids: Wm. B. Eerdmans Publishing Company, 1960. A brief introduction to the nature and purpose, study and defense of the Bible.

La Haye, Tim. *How to be Happy Though Married.* Wheaton: Tyndale House Publishers, 1968. Candid counsel on marriage and its problems. The kind of book that married couples and would-be-weds can profit from.

——————. *Spirit-Controlled Temperament.* Wheaton: Tyndale House Publishers, 1966. More superficial than Collins' *Search for Reality,* but a book which you should have in your library.

Lewis, Norman. *Triumphant Missionary Ministry in the Local Church.* Lincoln, Nebraska: Back to the Bible Broadcast, 1961. A book which every church member should read!

Little, Paul. *How to Give Away Your Faith.* Chicago: Inter-Varsity Press, 1966.

——————. *Know Why You Believe.* Chicago: Inter-Varsity Press, 1967. Two exceptional books by a man who writes from years of experience and who has counselled collegiates and people in all walks of life.

Loane, Marcus L. *The Place Called Calvary.* Grand Rapids: Zondervan Publishing House, 1968. A penetrating study of the crucifixion and Christ's last hours on the cross.

Luck, Coleman. *First Corinthians.* Chicago: Moody Press, 1958.

——————. *Second Corinthians.* Chicago: Moody Press, 1959. Two commendable commentaries which are ideal for adult study groups.

Martin, Alfred. *Isaiah: The Salvation of Jehovah.* Chicago: Moody Press, 1956. A worthy addition to the *Everyman's Bible Commentary* series.

Morris, Henry M. *Evolution and the Modern Christian.* Grand Rapids: Baker Book House, 1967. Perceptive studies by a hydraulic engineer and author of the excellent title *Twilight of Evolution.*

——————- and John C. Whitcomb, Jr. *The Genesis Flood.* Philadelphia: Presbyterian and Reformed Publishing Company, 1961. An excellent, indispensable treatment on the universality of the flood.

Murray, Andrew. *Absolute Surrender.* Chicago: Moody Press, n.d.

——————. *The Prayer Life.* Chicago: Moody Press, n.d.

——————. *The School of Obedience.* Chicago: Moody Press, n.d. Three heart-warming devotional books by a Dutch Reformed minister.

Narramore, Clyde M. *This Way to Happiness*. Grand Rapids: Zondervan Publishing House, 1964.

_____. *A Woman's World*. Grand Rapids: Zondervan Publishing House, 1966. Dr. Narramore has written several books for young people, among them *Young Only Once*. In these books he deals with the basic drives of all individuals and shows how to succeed in spite of one's circumstances.

Nederhood, Joel. *The Holy Triangle*. Grand Rapids: Baker Book House, 1970. A practical book on marriage and the family.

Orr, J. Edwin. *Faith That Makes Sense*. Valley Forge: Judson Press, 1962. A forthright, easy-to-read defense of the Christian faith. The book is well illustrated by incidents from the author's own experience.

Packer, James I. *God Speaks to Man: Revelation and the Bible*. Philadelphia: Westminster Press, 1966. A clear presentation of the doctrine of Revelation and the Bible.

Palmer, Bernard. *Brigade Boys and the Basketball Mystery*. Chicago: Moody Press, 1963. This book and the others in the *Boys Brigade* series will delight your youth!

_____. *Danny and Ron Orlis and the Mexican Jungle Mystery*. Chicago: Moody Press, 1965. The *Danny Orlis* series is ideal for grades 6-8.

_____, *Felicia Cartwright and the Case of the Black Phantom*. Chicago: Moody Press, 1968. An intriguing series for girls in grades 6-8.

_____ and Marjorie Palmer. *Pioneer Girls and the Dutch Mill Mystery*. Chicago: Moody Press, 1968. A *Pioneer Girls* series of equal calibre to the ones mentioned above.

Pfeiffer, Charles F. *Jerusalem Through the Ages*. Grand Rapids: Baker Book House, 1967. From the Baker Studies in Biblical Archaeology series.

Pinnock, Clark H. *Defense of Biblical Infallibility*. Philadelphia: Presbyterian and Reformed Publishing Company, 1967.

_____. *Set Forth Your Case*. Philadelphia: Presbyterian and Reformed Publishing Company, 1967.

Riess, Walter. *Before They Start to Leave*. St. Louis: Concordia Publishing House, 1967.

_____. *Teen-ager, the Bible Speaks to You*. St. Louis: Concordia Publishing House, 1959.

_____. *The Teen-ager You're Dating*. St. Louis: Concordia Publishing House, 1964. Three good books on teen-agers, the church, and the times in which they live.

Runyan, John. *Biff Norris and the Clue of the Angry Fisherman*. Chicago: Moody Press, 1966. The *Biff Norris* series, like the ones by Palmer, is specifically for boys and girls in grades 6-8.

Ryle, John Charles. *Warnings to the Churches.* London: Banner of Truth Trust, 1967. Timely messages to churches facing spiritual decline due to improper teaching.

Ryrie, Charles Caldwell. *The Holy Spirit.* Chicago: Moody Press, 1965. A simple, Biblically-oriented survey of the person and work of the Holy Spirit.

———. *Patterns for Christian Youth.* Chicago: Moody Press, n.d. Pertinent truths for today's teen-agers.

———. *Revelation.* Chicago: Moody Press, 1968. A plain, practical exposition of an often misunderstood book of the Bible.

Sanders, J. Oswald. *Cultivation of Christian Character.* Chicago: Moody Press, 1965.

Schaeffer, Francis A. *Pollution and the Death of Man.* Wheaton: Tyndale House Publishers, 1970. Gives the Christian perspective to our ecological problems.

Shedd, Charlie W. *Pastoral Ministry of Church Officers.* Richmond: John Knox Press, 1966. A handy "manual" for those engaged in the ministry of visitation.

Smith, Hannah Whitall. *Christian's Secret of a Happy Life.* Westwood, N.J.: Fleming H. Revell Company, n.d. An old work with a contemporary appeal.

———. *Everyday Religion.* Chicago: Moody Press, 1966. A reprint of a work designed to show how "piety in the home" is worked out in practice.

Spring, Gardiner. *Distinguishing Traits of Christian Character.* Philadelphia: Presbyterian and Reformed Publishing Company, 1967.

Stott, John R. W. *Basic Christianity.* Chicago: Inter-Varsity Press, 1958. A balanced treatment of Christ's person and man's need, and Christ's work and man's response.

Strachan, Kenneth R. *Inescapable Calling.* Grand Rapids: Wm. B. Eerdmans Publishing Company, 1968. A plain presentation of the missionary task of the church in the light of contemporary events and opportunities.

Strombeck, J. F. *Disciplined by Grace.* Chicago: Moody Press, 1946. Studies in Christian conduct.

Taylor, Kenneth N. *Bible in Pictures for Little Eyes.* Chicago: Moody Press, n.d.

———. *Devotions for the Children's Hour.* Chicago: Moody Press, 1959.

———. *Romans for the Family Hour.* Chicago: Moody Press, 1959.

.... *Stories for the Children's Hour.* Chicago: Moody Press, 1953. The best that money can buy!

Thomas, W. H. Griffith. *Christianity is Christ.* Chicago: Moody Press, 1965. An understandable presentation of the foundations upon which the Christain faith is built.

Towns, Elmer L. *Ministry to the Young Single Adult.* Grand Rapids: Baker Book House, 1971.

.... *Successful Youth Work.* Glendale, California: Gospel Light Publications, 1966.

.... *Teaching Teens.* Grand Rapids: Baker Book House, 1965.

Tozer, A. W. *Born After Midnight.* Harrisburg, Pa.: Christian Publications, Inc., 1964.

.... *Of God and Men.* Harrisburg, Pa.: Christian Publications, Inc., 1960.

.... *Root of the Righteous.* Harrisburg, Pa.: Christian Publications, Inc., 1955.

.... *That Incredible Christian.* Harrisburg, Pa.: Christian Publications, Inc., 1964. These messages ring with prophetic insight and unction and answer the need of our times.

Trench, R. C. *Notes on the Miracles of our Lord.* Grand Rapids: Baker Book House, 1949. A classic. This is widely acknowledged as being the most comprehensive and penetrating story of the subject in the English language.

Vos, Howard F. (ed.) *Can I Trust The Bible?* Chicago: Moody Press, 1963.

.... *Effective Bible Study.* Grand Rapids: Zondervan Publishing House, 1969. A handy manual on Bible study methods.

Wald, Oletta. *Joy of Discovery.* Minneapolis: Bible Banner Press, 1956.

Weiss, G. Christian. *Perfect Will of God.* Chicago: Moody Press, 1950. A challenging book . . . right down to the last page!

Wilson, Geoffrey B. *Romans.* London: Banner of Truth Trust, 1969.

Winter, David. *Christian's Guide to Church Membership.* Chicago: Moody Press, 1963.

Young, Edward J. *Thy Word is Truth.* Grand Rapids: Wm. B. Eerdmans Publishing Company, 1957. Indispensable!

10. Preparation of Materials

The arrival of books which have been ordered usually creates excitement. But what must be done with them? How do libraries keep records and prepare the books for use by the public? How are "accession" records kept, classification numbers worked out, book plates inserted, cards typed and the books made ready for circulation?

This chapter details a step-by-step approach to the subject of preparing materials for circulation. Many will be surprised to find how easy it is to begin a library.

When new books are received in a library they are generally protected by colorful book jackets or dust covers. Many church librarians prefer to retain these dust covers on the books. Because these paper dust covers wear very quickly, it is essential to cover them with plastic material to prolong their usefulness. Plastic covers may be purchased from any number of library supply houses. The most recent innovation is a plastic jacket which may be adjusted to fit books of different sizes. Some librarians, however, prefer to obtain sheets of plastic for book covers. This is invariably cheaper than buying adjustable book jackets. If the latter course is adopted, then the plastic is fitted over the book jacket and held in place with strips of 3M Magic Tape.

If the dust cover is retained, the call number should be lettered directly on the spine of the book as well as on the book jacket. This way, when the book jacket becomes worn, frayed and is discarded, the book will not have to be removed from circulation for lettering, because it will already have the call letters on it.

If the book jackets are removed, the biographical material about the author and the publisher's description of the book may be clipped from the dust cover and pasted inside the cover of the book. The rest of the jacket may be kept for use in a book display.

The Accession Record

The Accession Record may be kept in either a loose-leaf accession book purchased from a library supply house or in any other book ruled for that purpose (Figure 1). A loose-leaf book is most convenient for typing, and new pages can always be substituted for those which become worn or soiled.

An accession number is given to each new book as it is entered in the record, and this number is taken from the line on which the book is entered in the accession book. This number is never used again and so becomes unique to that particular book.

Date									
Accession Number	AUTHOR	TITLE		PUBLISHER	YEAR	SOURCE	COST	REMARKS	
51									
52									
53									
54									
55									
56									
57									
58									
59									
60									
61									
62									
63									
64									
65									
66									
67									
68									

Courtesy, Demco Educational Corp.

Accession Record

Figure 1

Each entry in the accession book consists of the author's last name, a brief title, the publisher, date of the book, the cost, and the source from which it was obtained. If there is more than one author, then use the last name of the first author mentioned on the title page. If no author is given on the title page, then the entry is made by the title. The date may be taken from the title page; and if no date is given, then the date may be taken from the information on the verso (reverse) of the title page and a small "c" placed before it to indicate that the copyright date is being used (e.g., c1970). If more than one date is found on the back of the title page, the last one is placed in the accession record. If no date is found, then "n.d." is used to indicate that there is no date. In the column labeled "Remarks" you may indicate the local Christian bookstore or the jobber from which the book was purchased.

The date on which the increase was made is placed in the space provided in the left-hand margin.

The accession number is lettered in ink inside the book on the page following the title page. Many libraries place the accession number about one inch from the top of the page and fairly close to the spine of the book.

Classification

Although many librarians develop their own system of classification, this task requires a specialist. For this reason it will be better if you follow a system which has already been found to work well. The Dewey Decimal Classification system is used by most public libraries and can be adapted for both large and small church libraries. It is the one which the authors have used in the churches in which they have started libraries, and also in their own personal libraries.

Each book in the library must be given a "call number." This number distinguishes the book from every other volume in the library. These call numbers are composed of two parts, (1) the classification number (often referred to as "class number"), and (2) the author number. Classification is always by subject. In order to ascertain the classification of a book, refer to the title page, the table of contents, and the preface. From this you should be able to deduce what the book is about. If you are still unsure of how to classify the book, scan certain chapters to gain an idea of the subject treated in the book.

Chapters 12 and 13 contain the basic information about the Dewey Decimal Classification system and a subject guide to the Dewey Decimal Classification system. By using the information from these two chapters you will be able to classify most of the books which you will receive in your library. Chapter 12 contains a breakdown of the 200 RELIGION section of the classification scheme which will enable you to classify commentaries, background material, books on doctrine, devotional works, surveys of pastoral practices and procedures, discussions on the nature and function of the church, books on church history and denominations, etc.

When you have established the classification number of the book, this number forms the top line of the call number.

To obtain the author number (the second line of the call number), consult the Cutter-Sanborn 3-figure author table (distributed by the H. R. Huntting Company, 300 Burnett Road, Chicopee Falls, Mass., $10).

To illustrate, if you were placing the book, *Major Bible Themes* by Lewis Sperry Chafer, in your library, you would assign it the number 230 because it deals with Bible doctrine. This is the class number. Now, consulting the Cutter table you would find that 433 is the numerical equivalent of the author's name. "C" being the first letter of his name (Chafer), the call number would be $\frac{230}{C433}$. To distinguish this book from Chafer's *Systematic Theology* you may wish to add to the Cutter number the first letter of the title. The Cutter number would then

Cars	321	Ces	421	Cher	521
Cart	322	Ceso	422	Chero	522
Carter	323	Cet	423	Cheru	523
Carter L	324	Cev	424	Ches	524
Carter S	325	Cey	425	Chest	525
Carth	326	Ch	426	Chet	526
Carti	327	Chabe	427	Chev	527
Carto	328	Chabo	428	Chevi	528
Cartw	329	Chabr	429	Chevr	529
Carv	331	Chac	431	Chey	531
Cary	332	Chad	432	Chi	532
Cary M	333	Chaf	433	Chich	533
Cas	334	Chai	434	Chif	534
Casan	335	Chais	435	Chil	535
Casat	336	Chal	436	Child	536
Case	337	Chall	437	Childs	537
Casen	338	Chalm	438	Chill	538
Casi	339	Chalo	439	Chin	539

Courtesy, R. A. Cutter

Sample of "Cutter" Numbers

Figure 2

read C433M for this book; while for Chafer's *Systematic Theology* it would read C4335S.

Should you desire any further information on Cutter numbers, we recommend *Book Numbers* by Bertha R. Barden (Chicago: American Library Association, 1937).

Biographies are treated differently from other books. Some librarians dispense with a number altogether and use a "B" instead of the Dewey Decimal Classification number, followed by the first three or four letters of the name of the biographee, the person about whom the book is written — *not* the author.

Suppose you choose to use "B" and dispense with numbers. If you were classifying a book on the life of D. L. Moody, the call number would appear like this:
B
MOOD ·

The Dewey Decimal Classification number for collective biographies is 920, and for individual biographies 921. Religious biographies (for missionaries and leaders of the church) is 922.

Should you choose to use 922 (biographical work of a church leader), it would look like this: $\frac{922}{\text{MOOD}}$.

But suppose you have two biographies of D. L. Moody, one by Pollock, the other by Findlay. Using either of the above methods you would be unable to distinguish between the books written by different authors about the same person. To overcome this deficiency some librarians use the first two letters of the name of the biographee and the first two letters of the author's name. This, however, is not very satisfactory.

The preferable way is to use the Cutter table for the name of the biographee rather than the author. Then the call number will read: $\frac{922}{\text{M817F}}$ or $\frac{922}{\text{M817P}}$ The 817 is the numerical equivalent for Moody. The first letter of the biographee's name precedes the number, and the first letter of the author's name follows it.

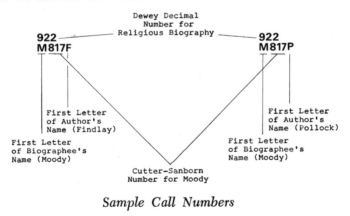

Sample Call Numbers

Figure 3

Classifying books on history, geography, travel, and literature can be a bit difficult. In order for you to be able to classify books in these areas successfully it may be necessary for you to enroll in a one-semester course at a college in your area. However, additional information on classification may be found in the 11th chapter of *The Abridged Dewey Decimal Classification System.* Should you wish to do some extra reading on the subject, *An Introduction to the Seventeenth Edition of Dewey Decimal Classification* by C. D. Batty (Hamden, Conn.: Shoe String, 1967), and *A Guide to the Use of the Dewey Decimal Classification* (Essex County, New York: Forest Press, 1962) will both be found helpful.

Once the call letters have been established they are penciled into the book in the upper right-hand corner of the page immediately after the cover of the book. They can then be referred to easily when someone types up the catalog cards.

Cataloging

An essential part of every library is a Dictionary Card Catalog. This consists of 3 x 5-inch cards on which is recorded information about each book in the library. Cataloging, therefore, is merely making a record of an item in the collection.

The card catalog consists of at least three cards per book. Essentially the same information appears on each of these three cards; however one deals specifically with the author and is filed under the author's name; on a second card the title is placed above the author's name and filed by that title; while the other deals with the subject found in the book and is filed under this subject. (If the book is concerned with more than one major subject, more than one subject card will be needed.) A separate card, identical to the author card, may be used as a Shelf List Card, but this is filed separately.

The easiest way to develop a card catalog is to order the cards from the Library of Congress in Washington, D.C. The Library of Congress order number which is usually found on the verso of the title page should be supplied with your order. The Library of Congress supplies its order forms free of charge. These forms must be used because the information is read by an optical reader. At the present time each set of cards supplied by the Library of Congress costs about 45 cents.

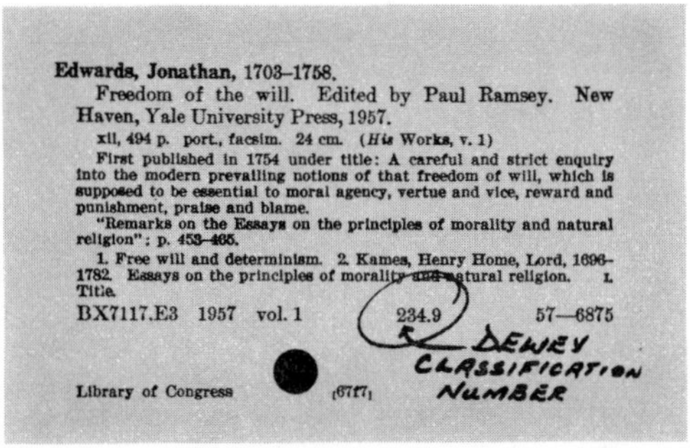

Edwards, Jonathan, 1703–1758.
Freedom of the will. Edited by Paul Ramsey. New Haven, Yale University Press, 1957.
xii, 494 p. port., facsim. 24 cm. (*His* Works, v. 1)
First published in 1754 under title: A careful and strict enquiry into the modern prevailing notions of that freedom of will, which is supposed to be essential to moral agency, vertue and vice, reward and punishment, praise and blame.
"Remarks on the Essays on the principles of morality and natural religion": p. 453–465.
1. Free will and determinism. 2. Kames, Henry Home, Lord, 1696–1782. Essays on the principles of morality and natural religion. I. Title.
BX7117.E3 1957 vol. 1 234.9 57—6875
Library of Congress ₍67f7₎

Sample Card from Library of Congress

Figure 4

If limitations within the library budget makes purchasing these cards out of the question, the best thing to do is to have an assistant type up the cards. Following are examples of each type of card and detailed instructions laid down by the American Library Association for typing each of them. More information regarding the layout of cards may be obtained from *Anglo-American Cataloging Rules* (Chicago: American Library Association, 1967), Chapter 6.

The primary purpose of the *author* or *main entry card* is to indicate the full name of the author; the year of his birth; and, if deceased, the year of his death. These dates may be omitted if the information is not readily available.

However, if the author's name is a very common one (e.g., Smith, John) you should try to obtain his date of birth to help distinguish him from someone else of the same name.

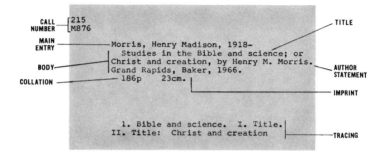

Author or Main Entry Card

Figure 5

Four lines down from the top of the card and nine spaces in from the left-hand edge (first indention) appears the author's name (last name first) which is obtained from the title page, year of birth, and, if deceased, year of death. In the event the book was authored by more than one person, the principal author is listed, or the editor or compiler. If the book was written by a committee, the main entry will bear the name of the committee or association.

Positioning this information in this manner allows enough space on the left-hand side for the call number, which should be typed in the top left-hand corner of every card in the card catalog.

Following the main entry is the body of the card, beginning eleven spaces in from the left edge of the card (second indention). The second and succeeding lines of the body of the card begin at first indention. The body of the card consists of the title, sub-title, author statement, editions statement, and imprint (the place of publication, the name of the publisher, and the date). Illustrations and forewords are included only if they appear on the title page. If this is the case, they go between the author statement and the editions statement.

Only the first letter of the title is capitalized unless other words in the title are proper nouns. If there is a sub-title, this comes immediately after the title and is separated from it by a comma, semi-colon, or colon, depending upon the rules of grammar. The title or sub-title is generally followed by a comma (when the title and/or subtitle is short), which is followed by the *author statement*. When the word "by" does not appear on the title page, it is enclosed in brackets. The author statement is always followed by a period.

If there is no author statement, the *editions statement* follows the title or sub-title. The editions statement is always placed in brackets if the information has to be taken from the verso of the title page. If the information is found on the title page the brackets are omitted. Periods or commas never follow brackets.

In the same paragraph, but leaving four spaces to separate it from the author or editions statement, the *imprint* follows — the place of publication, followed by a comma; the publisher, followed by a comma; the year of publication, followed by a period. If, however, the year of publication does not appear on the title page, then the date should be placed within brackets and in this case it is not preceded by a comma nor followed by a period.

Beginning a new paragraph at the second indention, the *collation* follows. This deals with the extent of the text (i.e. the number of pages), the illustrations, maps, and the height of the book in centimeters. When recording the number of pages, include the last numbered page of each section. For example, if the introduction or preface is numbered in Roman numerals, include the Roman figure as well as the Arabic number indicating the number of pages in the major contents.

If the book is in a series, the *series statement* follows, on the same line as the collation, but separated from it by four spaces. The title of the series is always placed in parentheses.

Notes, which follows the collation, are separated from the body of the card by a line. Although some libraries make a practice of putting notes on almost every card, this procedure is not necessary and consumes a lot of time. Notes refer to the first American edition of a book, or a translation of a book, or alert a reader to the fact that a book published in England under one title is available in America under another title — for example, F. F. Bruce wrote a work which was printed in England under the title, *This Is That.* When the book was published in the United States the title was changed to *New Testament Development of Old Testament Themes.* A note advising a patron of such a fact would be quite in order.

The *tracing* makes up the last entry on the card. It begins near the bottom of the card and at the second indention. It contains a record of all the headings (other than the main entry heading) where a card pertaining to this book may be found. Subject headings are listed by Arabic numerals, while added entries follow in Roman numerals. The subject headings relate to the content of the book. The added entries refer to joint authors or translators and the title. An indispensable aid in arriving at consistent logical subject headings is *Sears List of Subject Headings* by Bertha M. Frick (9th edition, ed. by Barber M. Westby. New York: H. W. Wilson Company, 1965). Other helpful books are *Descriptive Cataloging,* by James A. Taite and F. Douglas Anderson (Hamden, Conn.: Archon Books, 1968), and *Simple Library Cataloging,* by Susan Grey Akers (4th ed., Chicago: American Library Association, 1954). Special rules for cataloging related

works may be found in *Anglo-American Cataloging Rules,*
pp. 156-172 (#'s 108-119).

Figure 6, an author card for the book, *An Introduction
to Evangelical Christian Education,* edited by J. Edwards
Hakes, illustrates the rules discussed above.

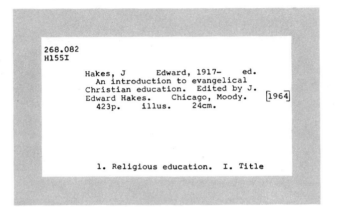

Author Card

Figure 6

Whenever the name of the author is incomplete space
is allowed in the author statement. This is done on the as-
sumption that sometime in the future you may be able to
complete the author's name for the main entry. The author
statement, however, must always reflect what is on the title page. The only exception to this rule is if the author
statement is an integral part of the title.

Titles like Sir, Dr., Ph.D., Professor of the Department
of Biblical Languages and Exegesis, etc., are generally
omitted from the card.

In the event a book has been authored by more than
one person and the words "by" and "and" do not appear
on the title page, these words are added but placed in
brackets.

Upon occasion you may find that more than one city is listed on the title page. If, for example, you find "London, New York, Paris" as the place of publication, in the imprint you will type the first city and, if this is not an American city, the first American city. The card, in this case, would read: London, New York. If, however, no place of publication is recorded, then put n.p. (for "no place") between brackets.

The *title card* (Figure 7) is designed to record the entry of the book in the catalog by title. It will be exactly the same as the author card except for one entry. Above the author entry and 13 spaces in from the left-hand edge of the card (third indention) the title will be typed.

```
268.082        An Introduction to Evangelical
H155I          Christian Education

        Hakes, J      Edward, 1917-      ed.
          An introduction to evangelical
        Christian education.  Edited by J.
        Edward Hakes.     Chicago, Moody    [1964]
          423p.     illus.    24cm.




             1. Religious education.  I. Title.
```

Title Card

Figure 7

The function of the *subject card* (Figure 8) or cards is to give a comprehensive subject index to the contents of the book. The subject card will be identical to Figure 7 with one exception. The subject heading will appear in capital letters in place of the title. A separate card will be typed for each major subject treated in the book.

```
268.082
H155I        Religious Education

        Hakes, J          Edward, 1917-      ed.
        An introduction to evangelical
        Christian education.  Edited by J.
        Edward Hakes.    Chicago, Moody   [1964]
            423p.    illus.    24cm.




          1. Religious education.  I. Title.
```

Subject Card

Figure 8

As mentioned earlier, most librarians also keep a Shelf List Card in a separate file. This card is identical to the main entry or author card but it is filed by "call number." It is checked when new books are added to the library to insure that call numbers are not duplicated.

The other cards are filed in alphabetical order. In the early stages of your library's development it will be a simple matter to file these cards correctly. However, as more cards are added to your file, you will want to read the *ALA Rules for Filing Catalog Cards* by Pauline A. Seely (2d ed., Chicago: American Library Association, 1968) to make sure that you are placing these cards in the correct order.

Preparation for circulation

Before the books can be allowed to circulate, book cards (Figure 9) and book pockets (Figure 10) must be prepared. The call letters should be typed in the left-hand corner of the book card, and the accession number in the right-hand corner. This is followed by the author's name and the title.

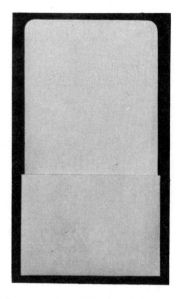

Book Card

Figure 9

Book Pocket

Figure 10

Book pockets should also be prepared and pasted in the center of the inside back cover of the book.

Date due slips are then pasted on the last page of the book facing the book pocket. These generally have a narrow gummed surface across the top of the back. You may find that these date due slips come detached rather easily. It is advisable, therefore, that these be glued on with additional paste, rather than water. If there is reading material on the last page of the book, the date due slip should be pasted across the top margin of the page, or else an inch or two above the book pocket.

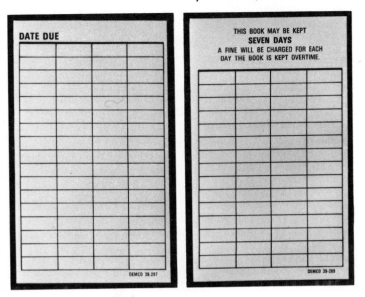

Courtesy, Demco Educational Corp.

Date Due Slips

Figure 11

Before the books are finally ready for placement on the shelves, it is necessary for them to be lettered with the call number on the outside of the book. The easiest way to do this is to obtain gummed labels which are supplied on wax paper. These can easily be inserted into a typewriter and after the call letters have been typed they are peeled off the wax paper backing, and attached to the spine of the book approximately two inches from the base.

You may prefer to write the call letters on the book spine with pen and ink. This should be done only by someone able to print neatly. White ink should be used on dark-colored books and black waterproof ink on light-colored books. Should the cover of the book be rough, or if the nature of the ink be such that it runs or will not adhere to the surface of the book, you will first need to glue book cloth in the appropriate spot before the lettering can be done.

Some libraries use an electric stylus (Figure 12). These may be purchased from library supply houses who will also supply you with the special colored transfer paper. The stylus must be plugged into an electrical outlet (110 volts) and heated before applying it to the transfer paper.

Courtesy, Demco Educational Corp.

Electric Stylus

Figure 12

Many books and pamphlets are too thin to be lettered across the spine. Where the spine is thick enough the call numbers may be placed vertically instead of horizontally. If, however, the book is too thin for this, the call letters should be placed on the front cover of the book, two inches from the bottom and about an inch from the spine.

The marks of ownership should be stamped on each book. Each library should have its own rubber stamp (Figure 13) with its name on it, e.g.,

> LIBRARY
> GRACE BIBLE CHURCH
> DULUTH

Rubber Stamp
Figure 13

The marks of identification should be placed on the title page, page 77 (or some other page), and across the bottom of the book pocket. Some librarians also stamp the marks of ownership on the edges of the book as a further measure to discourage people from taking the books.

The book is now ready for placement on the shelf. Properly shelved books should occupy only two thirds of each shelf. This leaves room for future expansion. Books should be arranged on the shelves from left to right in accordance with the call numbers. The spines should be flush with the edge of each shelf, and a metal book support (Figure 14) will insure that the books stand upright.

Book Supports
Figure 14

Shelf labels containing the classification number and the subject headings will assist readers in locating books easily and quickly. These shelf labels together with the metal holders (Figure 15) may be ordered from a library supply house. A U-shaped holder which slips over the shelves is advisable, for these may be changed easily and quickly; whereas fixed shelf labels are not so easily moved around.

Courtesy, Gaylord Bros., Inc.

Shelf Label Holder

Figure 15

The preparation of books (and other materials) for circulation will take time, but if done well it will be worth the effort. Well labeled, neat-looking books are a delight to a librarian's heart. However, the library is neither a museum nor an art gallery. The books are not there to collect dust nor are they there solely to be admired. They are there to be read — *circulated* among the teachers in the Sunday school and the people of the church so that their message can bring blessing and enrichment to those who read them.

11. The Circulation of Materials

All of the work in preparing the book for a place on the library shelves is with the view to having it used by people within the church. The circulation of materials, therefore, is of vital importance in all libraries. Before books can be checked out, however, it will be necessary for the library committee to set up a *library policy*. A policy must be developed as to how materials are to be circulated and for what length of time; what procedures will be adopted for circulation of books among children in the Sunday school, their parents, and the teachers; what will be the policy with regard to overdue books and fines; and what course of action should be adopted in the event of a book being lost.

Inasmuch as policies vary with librarians, institutions, and situations, policies of this nature must be developed by the committee and then adhered to.

It is strongly advised that a routine for each type of material in the library be developed and taught to all who assist in the library. Quite obviously the policy for checking out flannelgraph material or an overhead projector (which may only be used once and then returned to the library) will vary from the routine for checking out a book which will be taken outside of the church precincts for a period of two to three weeks. The routine developed for books, periodicals, projectors and screens, flannelgraph material, and other audio-visual aids should be followed consistently and in the same manner regardless of the time of day, the person working at the desk, and who it is that wishes to borrow the materials. Nothing can confuse library organization or be more disconcerting than to find a miscellany of notes relating to books and materials that have been inconsistently checked out. A good routine will eliminate this frustration and insure that each item is checked out in a uniform manner.

Now, what about a system, some way to organize the circulation of books and materials? What personnel will you have helping you in the library? How much time and attention will you be able to devote to "on-the-spot" routine matters? The system presented in this chapter is suggested because it is easy to follow, works well, and requires very little direct supervision.

Checking Out Books

Each book in the collection should have a book card (Figure 9) in the book pocket (Figure 10). Regular books, which circulate for two to three weeks, have *white* cards, whereas other books which may be needed by several teachers during one quarter and are restricted in their circulation during that quarter may have pink- or blue-colored cards. This latter type may be classified as "reserve" books and more will be said about them later.

Regular books, those which are equipped with white cards and circulated for a period of two to three weeks, are to be brought to the circulation desk where the reader will remove the card from the book pocket, write his name on the first vacant line, and then stamp the date due on the card beside his name *and* on the first vacant space on the date due slip (Figure 11) on the inside back cover of the book. The card is then placed in a box or tray with other cards pertaining to other books which have been checked out on that same day.

These cards then are filed in trays specially designed to

hold book cards (Figure 16). These trays are placed at the check-out desk for use in circulation trays.

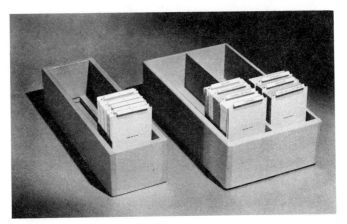

Card Trays

Figure 16

Date due stamps (Figure 17) should be changed each time the library is open for business. These stamps should reflect the date when materials will be due back in the library and can be differentiated from one another by choosing daters with different colored handles or by attaching a label or a piece of adhesive tape to the flat surface on the top of the handle. These daters may then be labeled "three weeks," "reserve," and "one day" for visual-aid equipment. The color of the label may also be made to conform to the color of the book card. In this way a person who has a white card in the pocket of a book will use a date due stamp with a white label on it. A person checking out other material with either a blue or pink card will use a date due stamp with a blue or pink label on it. This should avoid confusion.

Courtesy, Demco Educational Corp.

Date Due Stamps

Figure 17

Reference Materials

Books such as encyclopedias, manuals on different Biblical topics which will be in constant use during one particular quarter, concordances, and Bible atlases may be classified as reference material by the librarian and the committee. Because of the heavy demand for books of this nature, circulation may be limited to one week (Sunday to Sunday) instead of the usual two to three weeks.

Checking In Books

This procedure is referred to in some library manuals as "discharging books." Regardless of the period of time a book has been out, the procedure for processing its return should always be the same. The assistant at the desk should check the date due on the date due slip inside the back cover of the book. From the date due information the assistant will be able to find a card which has the corresponding date and is filed in the circulation file. He will then return the book card to the pocket and, depending upon the library procedure, stamp it with the date on which it was returned. The pertinent information should be checked to insure that the call letters, author, and title are the same as the book being returned. If not, the assistant will realize that he has the wrong book card and will check further to find the right one. In this way many problems in circulation will be prevented and the perplexity of having two books with wrong cards in their pockets will be eliminated.

If the assistant notices that the book is being returned late, the fine should be assessed immediately and the money paid. If this is made a routine method the necessity of handling over-due fines will be prevented.

When once the book has been checked in it should be placed on a book truck or shelf with other books that are ready to be integrated back into the collection. One person should be delegated the responsibility of placing books back on the shelves each time the library opens. This will prevent the accumulation of a large backlog of books for shelving and insure that the books are readily accessible to the readers.

Renewals

The problem of renewals and their frequency should be solved by the library committee. Some church libraries solve the problem of renewals by not allowing any. The philosophy behind this is that if a reader has not finished reading a book within a two- or three-week period it is unlikely that he will complete it if allowed extra time. This, however, is a somewhat harsh ruling, for even the best of readers sometimes find that the pressure of other affairs and events prevents him or her from completing a book on schedule. It would perhaps be better to renew the book for a further two weeks. Books should only be renewed when the book itself is present. This will enable the assistant to restamp the date due card and the date due slip and thus facilitate its return to the library.

The procedure by which a book is renewed will then be almost identical with the manner in which it is checked out and the date due card will be restamped with the new date on it and filed in the appropriate place.

Overdue Books

Whenever a borrower fails to return a book on time, a card (Figure 18) reminding him of his omission should be mailed to him, or he should be contacted by telephone. A telephone call will, however, invariably result in a request for a renewal of the book, and this may violate a policy of not renewing books without having the date due slip stamped with a new date due. All things considered, a postcard reminding a borrower that the book is due is the best way of handling the problem.

Courtesy, Demco Educational Corp.

Overdue Cards

Figure 18

Typing of New Cards

Whenever the circulation assistant notices that the last line of a book card has been used by a reader, the assistant should route the book through to the person who is responsible for typing new book cards. This may be the same person who initially was responsible for the processing of materials prior to their being placed in the library. When once the new book card has been typed up and placed in the book, the old card should be torn up and discarded. The book is then ready for shelving.

Reserve Books

It quite frequently happens that a book which is in great demand must be reserved for a reader. When this arises a card specially designed for the purpose should be made out and signed by the person requesting the reserve (Figure 19). The assistant will then need to search the circulation file for the book card and attach the reserve request to the back of the card with a paper clip. This should be sufficient to call the assistant's attention to the reserve when the book is returned. If a reserve request has been attached to the book card, no further renewal should be granted to the former borrower.

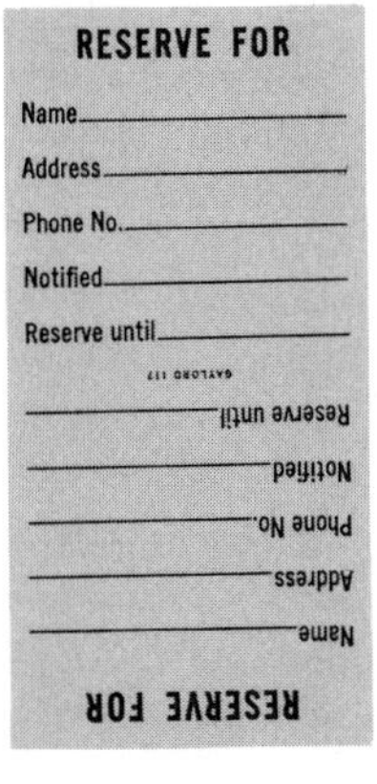
RESERVE FOR

Name__________

Address__________

Phone No.__________

Notified__________

Reserve until__________

GAYLORD 117

Reserve until__________

Notified__________

Phone No.__________

Address__________

Name__________

RESERVE FOR

Reserve Book Cards

Figure 19

Courtesy, Gaylord Bros., Inc.

Upon the return of the book the would-be borrower who has filed the reserve card should be notified (by postcard, telephone call, or memo placed in a church box) that the book has come in and asked to call at the library as soon as possible. The book should then be placed in a special place where reserve books are kept and held until the reader who has received the notice has a chance to come into the library. If, after about a week, the would-be borrower has not called, a further notice may be sent to him or his request may be canceled and the book placed on the shelves for regular circulation.

Non-Book Materials

Materials in the category of audio-visual aids and/or equipment pose a problem in circulation because in many instances it is not practical to provide non-book materials with book cards and pockets. Materials such as flannelgraphs, pictures, or transparencies, which may be kept in manila envelopes can easily have book pockets and date due slips attached to the envelopes. This will facilitate the checking out of these materials. For other materials where a book pocket cannot be attached (e.g. slide projectors and screens, tape recorders and record players, see Figure 20) a separate card should be kept in a special place at the reserve desk. The person requesting the loan of this equipment may then sign for the audio-visual material. Further information on the circulation of materials may be found in Leila H. Kirkwood's book *Charging Systems*, volume 2, part 3 of *The State of the Library Art*, edited by Ralph R. Shaw (New Brunswick: Rutgers University Press, 1961).

These elementary procedures will enable you to *begin* to organize your church library.

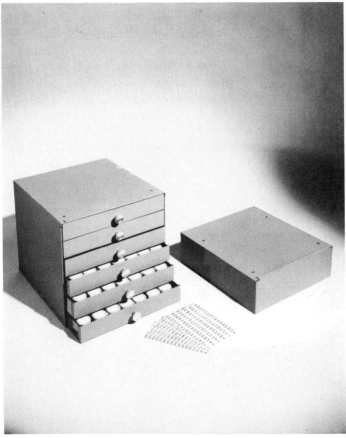

Courtesy, Demco Educational Corp.

Filmstrip Cabinet and Base

Figure 20

12. An Introduction to the Dewey Decimal Classification System

In Chapter 10 the process of preparing books for integration into the library was discussed. The Dewey Decimal Classification system was suggested because it is the most appropriate system and it is easy to use. This chapter will give an idea of the way the Dewey system works and how the books may be classified in an orderly manner. The following chapter contains a Subject Guide to the Dewey system. Use either of these chapters in doing your early classification of books.

The Dewey Decimal Classification system was first developed by Melvin Dewey in 1873. Since then it has gone through many editions and has been enlarged and expanded to its present size. The basic idea behind the development of Dewey's system is to analyze knowledge from a *human* point of view. The entire system is summarized in the chart which follows.

No.	Answering the Question . . .	Subject Matter
000		General Works
100	Who am I?	Philosophy and Psychology
200	Who made me?	Religion
300	What about other people?	Social Sciences and Education

400	How may I communicate with others?	Philology and Language
500	How may I understand the world around me?	Science
600	How may I use what I have learned about nature and science?	Applied Arts and Sciences
700	How may I enjoy my leisure time?	Fine Arts and Recreation
800	How may I pass on to posterity what I have learned?	Literature
900	How may I leave a record for the future?	History, Biography, and Geography

We shall be concerned mainly with the 200 section. This section is divided into ten areas as follows:

200 — Religion

210 — Natural Theology

220 — Bible

230 — Doctrine, Theology

240 — Christian Life

250 — Homiletic, Pastoral

260 — Christian Church

270 — Church History

280 — Denominations and Sects

290 — Non-Christian Religions

Each of these areas is further subdivided into related subjects within the groups, and together they form a comprehensive outline of all the various facets of Christianity. For more complete material you may consult the unabridged edition of the Dewey Decimal Classification system (1 vol. ed.) or the unabridged two-volume edition. For your convience the most important subdivisions are provided for your guidance and easy reference. The material is taken from the 17th edition of the Dewey Decimal Classification system and is used by permission of the publishers. Changes in the system are indicated in italics.

200	**RELIGION**		.7	Commentaries on the Old Testament
.1	Philosophy of Religion		.9	Geography, History, Chronology of Old Testament
.19	Psychological Aspects of Religion			
203	**Dictionaries, Encyclopedias, Concordances**		.91	Geography
205	**Journals, Magazines**		.92	Old Testament Biography
210	**Natural Religion**		.93	Archaeology of the Old Testament
211	**Knowledge of God**			
212	**Nature of God**		.95	History
213	**Creation**		**222**	**Historical Books**
215	**Science and Religion**		.1	Pentateuch (Five Books of Moses)
.5	Geology			
.6	Paleontology		.11	Genesis
.7	Anthropological and Biological Sciences		.12	Exodus
220	**Bible**			For Ten Commandments, see 222.16
.12	Canon			
.13	Inspiration		.13	Leviticus
.14	Authorship		.14	Numbers
.15	Prophetic Message		.15	Deuteronomy
.2	Concordances		.16	Ten Commandments
.3	Dictionaries, Encyclopedias		.2	Joshua
			.3	Judges
.4	Original Texts, Versions		.35	Ruth
			.4	Samuel
.5	Modern Versions		.5	Kings
.6	Interpretation		.6	Chronicles
.61	Introduction		.7	Ezra
.64	Typology		.8	Nehemiah
.7	Commentaries on the Whole Bible		.9	Esther
			223	**Poetic Books**
.8	Special Subjects		.1	Job
.9	Geography, History, Chronology		.2	Psalms
			.7	Proverbs
.92	Collective Biography		.8	Ecclesiastes
.93	Archaeology		.9	Song of Solomon
.95	History		**224**	**Prophetic Books**
221	**Old Testament**		.1	Isaiah
			.2	Jeremiah

.3 Lamentations
.4 Ezekiel
.5 Daniel
.6 Hosea
.7 Joel
.8 Amos
.91 Obadiah
.92 Jonah
.93 Micah
.94 Nahum
.95 Habakkuk
.96 Zephaniah
.97 Haggai
.98 Zechariah
.99 Malachi
225 New Testament
.9 Geography, History, Chronology
.91 Geography
.92 New Testament Biography
.93 Archaeology of the New Testament
.95 History
226 Gospels and Acts
.1 Harmonies of the Gospels
.2 Matthew
.3 Mark
.4 Luke
.5 John
.6 Acts of the Apostles
.7 Miracles
.8 Parables
.9 Lord's Prayer
227 Epistles
.1 Romans
.2 I Corinthians
.3 II Corinthians
.4 Galatians

.5 Ephesians
.6 Philippians
.7 Colossians
.8 Other Pauline Epistles
.81 I Thessalonians
.82 II Thessalonians
.83 I Timothy
.84 II Timothy
.85 Titus
.86 Philemon
.87 Hebrews
.9 Catholic (*General*) Epistles
.91 James
.92 I Peter
.93 II Peter
.94 I John
.95 II John
.96 III John
.97 Jude
228 Revelation
230 Doctrine, Theology
231 God, Trinity, Godhead
.1 God the Father
.3 Holy Spirit
.4 Attributes
.5 Providence
.6 Love and Wisdom
.7 Divine Law
232 Jesus Christ, *Christology*
.1 Incarnation and Messiahship
.3 Atonement
.4 Sacrifice
.5 Resurrection
.6 Second Coming
.8 Divine-Human Nature
.95 Public Life
.954 Teachings

.956 Transfiguration
.957 Last Supper
.96 Passion and Death
.962 Trial and Condemnation
.963 Crucifixion and Death
.964 Burial
.97 Resurrection, Appearances, Ascension
233 **Man**
.1 Grace
.2 Faith
.3 Redemption
.4 Regeneration
.5 Repentance
.6 Obedience
.7 Justification
.8 Sanctification
.9 Predestination, Free Will
235 **Angels, Angelology**
.3 Angels
.4 Devil, Demons
236 *Prophecy*
.3 *Signs of the Times, End of Church Age*
.4 *Second Advent of Christ, Rapture*
.5 *Tribulation*
.6 *Millennial Kingdom*
.7 *Final Judgment*
.8 *Miscellaneous*
.9 *Eternal State*
237 *Future State*
.1 *Death, Intermediate State*
.12 *False Views of Death*
.2 *Immortality, Eternal Life*

.3 *Resurrection, (General Discussion of)*
.4 *Judgments, (General Discussion of)*
.5 *Heaven*
.6 *Hell*
.9 *Punishment, Rewards*
238 **Creeds and Confessions**
239 **Apologetics,** *Defense of Christianity*
240 **Devotional Books,** *Christian Life, Character*
241 **Christian Ethics**
245 **Hymns**
248 *Prayer*
.3 *Personal Bible Study*
.4 Conduct of Christian Life
249 **Christian Family Worship**
250 **Pastoral Theology**
251 **Preaching, Homiletics**
252 **Sermons**
253 **Pastor**
.2 *Personal Life*
.5 Counseling
254 **Church Administration**
.5 Membership
.7 Buildings and Equipment
.8 Finance
260 **Christian Church**
261.7 **Church and State**
262 **Government of the Church**

.1 *Leaders, Elders, Deacons, etc.*

.2 *Authority of the Church*

.9 *Discipline in the Church*

263 *Sunday, Sabbath*

264 **Public Worship**
  .1 Prayer
  .2 Music

265 *Ordinances, Sacraments*
  .1 Baptism
  .2 Confirmation
  .3 Lord's Supper, Communion, Eucharist
  .5 Marriage

266 **Missions**
  .022 Home
  .023 Foreign
  .025 Medical
  .09 Missionary Stories

267 **Association for Religious Work** (e.g., Y.W.C.A, Gideons, Salvation Army)

268 *Christian Education*[1]
  .1 Administration
  .2 Buildings and Equipment
  .3 Personnel
  .4 Teaching Departments, Divisions
  .432 Children's Divisions (ages 1-12)

.433 Young People's Division

.434 Adult Division

.435 Home Departments

.5 Records and Rules

.6 Methods of Instruction

269 *Revivals*

270 *History of the Christian Church*

272 **Persecutions**

273 **Heresies**

280 **Denominations and Sects**
  .1 Ecumenical Movement

282 **Roman Catholic Church**

283 **Anglican Churches**

284 **Protestant Denominations**
  .1 Lutheran Churches

285 **Presbyterian** *and Reformed Churches*

286 **Baptist, Disciples of Christ, Adventist Churches**

287 **Methodist Churches**

288 **Unitarianism**

289 **Other Denominations and Sects**
  .3 Mormons
  .5 Christian Science
  .6 Quakers, Society of Friends
  .7 Mennonites

[1]See pages 37-38 of the *Rossin-Dewey Subject List* for a detailed subdivision of the 268 category. Obtainable from Donald F. Rossin, 150 Jackson Avenue North, Hopkins, Minnesota 55343.

.9	Others	296	Judaism
290	Non-Christian Re-	297	Mohammedanism
	ligions	299	Other Non-Christian
294	Hinduism, Buddhism		Religions

When classifying a new book determine the contents from a careful survey of the table of contents and the preface. Then check the Dewey list for an appropriate classification. For example, if you are classifying *Conquest and Crisis* by John J. Davis (Baker), you would first check the title page, then the table of contents, and finally the preface. Your conclusion would probably be that it deals with the books of *Joshua, Judges,* and *Ruth;* is highlighted with archaeological information; and pays close attention to chronology. This would be correct. Obviously you cannot give it a classification for all *three* books and so you would probably choose the first book, *Joshua.* On checking the Dewey tables you find that *Joshua* is classified as 222.2. You are now free to check for the author number in the "Cutter" tables. Once this has been found your book has been classified.

Now you may record the book in the Subject Index, under *Judges* and *Ruth.* The simplest method is to make out two extra subject cards and mark the one JUDGES and the other RUTH. This will insure that readers requiring material on either of these books can trace the material through the subject headings.

Now for the *Subject Index* . . .

13. Dewey Subject Guide for Easy Classification

In the preceding chapter we introduced you to the Dewey Decimal Classification system and showed how Melvin Dewey had sought to bring the whole realm of man's knowledge within the scope of his classification system. We then introduced you to one of the divisions within his system, the section which you will be using the most in classifying books for your library: 200 RELIGION. Now, you need a condensed subject guide containing the classification numbers for each subject.

When classifying a book the first and most important task is finding out the subject matter of the book. Once this has been done a relative index such as the one in this chapter will prove invaluable to you in finding out where the book belongs as far as the subject classification is concerned. Once again the subjects found in italics differ from the Dewey system, but this in no way impairs the value of Melvin Dewey's work.

Acts of the Apostles	226.6	Apocrypha	229
Adventists	286.7	Apologetics	239
Agnosticism	211	Archaeology, Biblical	220.93
Alcohol, -ism	178	—of the N.T.	225.93
Amos	224.8	—of the O.T.	221.93
Amusements	175	Associations, Religious	267
Angels, Angelology	235	Astronomy	520
Anger	179	Atheism	211
Animism	290	*Atlas, Bible*	220.9
Antichrist	235.4	Atlas, General	910

Atonement 232.3
Authority of the
Bible 220.1

Baptism 265.1
Baptist churches 286
Bible—Archaeology 220.93
—Authority 220.1
—Geography 220.92
—Canon 220.12
—Chronology 220.94
—Commentaries 220.7
—Concordances 220.2
—Criticism 220.6
—Dictionaries 220.3
—General works 220
—Geography 220.9
—Hermenuetics 220.6
—History 220.95
—Inspiration . 220.13
—Introductions 220.61
—Introductions (NT) 225.61
—Introductions (OT) 221.61
—Manners, Customs 220.96
—Names 220.97
—Special topics 220.8
—Stories for
children 268.6
—Typology 220.6
—Versions 220.5
Bible and science 239.8
Biography—General 920
—Specific character 921
—Biblical 220.92
—New Testament 225.92
—Old Testament 221.92

Calvary 232.4
Catechisms 238

Children's stories 268.6
Christ, Christology 232
Christian doctrine 230
Christian education 268
Christian ethics 241
Christian evidences 239
Christian life 240
Christian Science 289.5
Chronicles 222.6
Church, Christian 260
Church and state 261.7
Church finances 254
Church history 270
Church membership 265.2
Church music 264.2
Church ordinances 265
Church polity 262
Church union, unity 280
Church work 260
Colossians 227.7
Communion, Lord's
Supper 265.3
Communism 335.4
Comparative religions 290
Confirmation 265.2
Congregational
churches 285.8
Conscience 171.6
Corinthians, First 227.2
Corinthians, Second 227.3
Counseling, pastoral 258
Creation 213
Creeds 238
Crime, criminology 364
Cross of Christ 232.3
Cults 289, 290
Cyclopedias of the
Bible 220.3
—General 030

Daily Vacation Bible		Exodus	222.12
School	268.7	Ezekiel	224.4
Dancing	175	Ezra	222.7
Daniel	224.5		
Deacons, Deaconesses	262.15	Faith	234.2
Death	236.1	Fall (of man)	233.1
Decalogue	222.16	Family ethics	173
Deluge, Flood	*222.113*	Family devotions	249
Demons, Demonology	235.4	*Flood*	*222.113*
Denominations	280	Forgiveness	234
Devil, Satan	235.47	Free will	234.9
Deuteronomy	222.15	Future state	237
Devotional books			
and life	240	Galatians	227.4
Disciples of Christ	286.6	Gambling	175
Divine healing	265.8	Genesis	222.11
Divorce	173	Geography—Bible	220.9
Doctrinal theology	230	—General	910
Doubt (see Faith)	234.2	Gideons	267
Drinking	178	Giving, Stewardship	254
Drugs	178	God	231
		Gospels	226
Easter	232.5	—Harmonies	226.1
Ecclesiastes	223.8	Grace	234.1
Education	370	Greek Language—	
—Christian	268	New Testament	480
Ephesians	227.5		
Epistles, Paul's	227	Habakkuk	224.95
Eschatology,		Haggai	224.97
Prophecy	236	Happiness	171
Esther	222.9	Healing, divine	265.8
Eternal Life	234	Heaven	237.4
Eternity	236.9	Hebrews	227.87
Ethics—Christian	241	Hell	237.5
—General	170	Heresies	273
Etiquette	395	History—Bible	220.95
Eucharist	265.3	—Church	270
Evangelism	253	—General	900
Evil (see Sin)	233.2	Holiness, Sanctifi-	
Evolution	213	cation	234.8

Holy Spirit	231.3		Joshua	222.2
Home, Family	173		Judaism	296
Homiletics	251		Jude	227.97
Honesty	174		Judges	222.3
Hosea	224.6		Justification	234.7
Humility	179			
Hymnology	245		Kings	222.5

Illustrations, sermonic	251		Lamentations	224.3
Immortality	237.2		Leviticus	222.13
Infidelity	211		Logic	160
Inspiration	220.13		Lord's Prayer	226.9
Isaiah	224.1		Lord's Supper	265.3
			Love	177
James	227.91		Love, Christian	248
Jeremiah	224.2		Luke	226.4
Jesus Christ—			Lutherans	284.1
Atonement	232.3		Lying	177
—Birth, Incarnation	232.1			
—Burial	232.964		Magazines, Journals	
—Christology	232		—General	050
—Crucifixion	232.963		—Religious	205
—Deity, humanity	232.8		Malachi	233
—Life of	232.9		Manners and customs	
—Messiahship	232.1		—*Bible*	220.96
—Passion	232.96		—General	390
—Resurrection			Matthew	226.2
(Doctrine of)	232.5		Methodists	287
—Resurrection			Micah	224.93
(Event of)	232.97		Millennium	236.6
—Second coming	232.6		Miracles	226.7
—Temptation	232.952		*Missionary stories*	*268.6*
—Transfiguration	232.956		Missions—City	**266.21**
Job	223.1		—Foreign	
Joel	224.7		—General	266
John—Epistles, First	227.94		—Home	
—Epistles, Second	227.95		Mohammedanism	297
—Epistles, Third	227.96		Mormonism	289.3
Gospel	226.5		Music, Religious	245, 264.2
Jonah	224.92		Nahum	224.94

Nehemiah	222.8	Preaching	251
New Testament		Predestination,	
—Biography	225.92	Free will	234.9
—Commentaries	225.7	Presbyterian churches	285.1-6
—General works	225	Priesthood, Levitical	222.1
—Geography	225.9	Prohibition	178
—Introductions	225.61	Proverbs	223.7
—Versions, modern	225.5	Psalms	223.2
Numbers	222.14	Pseudopigrapha	229
Obadiah	224.91	Rationalism	211
Obedience	234.6	Redemption	234.3
Occultism	133	Regeneration	234.4
Old Testament		Repentance	234.5
—General works	221	Reformation	270.6
—Versions, modern	221.5	Reformed churches	285.7
Ordinances, Church	265	Religion and science	215
		Religions, Compara-	
Paganism	290	tive	290
Palestine, History		Religious education	268
and Geography	220.91	—Symbolism	220.64
Papacy	282	—Unity	280
Parables	226.8	Resurrection, Christ	232.5
Parents	173	—Believers	237.3
Pastoral problems	250	Revelation	228
—theology	250	Revivals	269
Pastor's wife	259	Roman Catholic	
Pedagogy, Religious	268	Church	282
Pentateuch	222.1	Romans	227.1
Persecution	272	Ruth	222.35
Peter, First	227.92		
Peter, Second	227.93	Sabbath	263
Philemon	227.86	Sacraments	265
Philippians	227.6	Salvation	234
Philosophy, General	100	Samuel, Books of	222.4
—Religious	201	Sanctification	234.8
Prayer, Family	249	Satan	235.47
—Private	248	Science and Religion	215
—Public	264.1	Scriptures, Bible	220
Prayer meetings	264.1	Sermons	252

Sin	233.2	Thessalonians, Second	227.82
Song of Solomon	223.9	Timothy, First	227.83
Spiritism, Spiritualism	133	Timothy, Second	227.84
Stewardship	254	Tithe, Tithing	254
Stories—Bible and		Titus	227.85
religious	*268.6*	Tobacco	178
Suffering	242	Trinity	231
Sunday observance	263		
Synagogues	296	Unbelief	211
Systematic theology	230	Unitarianism	288
		United States,	
Tabernacle	*222.123*	Religious history	277.3
Temperance	178		
Temptation	233.21	*Vacation Bible School*	*268.7*
Ten Commandments	221.16	Virgin Birth	232.1
Theism	211		
Theology	230	Zechariah	224.98
Thessalonians, First	227.81	Zephaniah	224.96

Bibliography

Buder, Christine. *How to Build a Church Library.* St. Louis: Bethany Press. 1955. 60p. ($1.25)

Church Library Development Plan, Stages 1 and 2. Nashville: Broadman Supplies. 1968. 70p. ($2.95)
Church Library Development Plan, Stage 3. Nashville: Convention Press. 161p. ($4.50)

Guide to Parish Libraries. (Parish Library and Bookshop Conference 1960) New York: The Seabury Press. n.d. 32p. ($1.00)

Johns, Erwin E. *The Key to a Successful Church Library.* Minneapolis: Augsburg Publishing House. 1967. 56p. ($1.50)
Johnson, Marian S. *Promoting Your Church Library.* Minneapolis: Augsburg Publishing House. 1968. 48p. ($3.50)

Newton, Charlotte. *Church Library Manual.* Privately printed and distributed by the author, Charlotte Newton, 892 Prince Avenue, Athens, Georgia 30601. 1964. 21p. ($1.25)
Newton, LaVose W. *Church Library Handbook.* Portland, Ore.: Multnomah Press. 1971. 145p. ($3.95)

Schneider, Rev. Vincent P. (ed) *The Parish and Catholic Lending Library Manual.* Haverford, Pa.: Catholic Library Association. 1965. 64p. ($1.50)
Sunday School Library. Springfield, Mo.: National Sunday School Department, Assemblies of God. n.d. 6-page pamphlet.

Directory of Publishers

Abingdon Press
 201 Eighth Avenue, South, Nashville, Tenn. 37202
American Library Association
 50 East Huron Street, Chicago, Ill. 60611
Archon Books
 See The Shoe String Press
Assemblies of God
 National Sunday School Department, 1445 Boonville, Springfield, Missouri 65802
Association Press
 291 Broadway, New York, N. Y. 10007
Augsburg Publishing House
 426 South Fifth Street, Minneapolis, Minn. 55415

Back to the Bible Broadcast
 Box 233, Lincoln, Neb. 68501
Baker Book House
 1019 Wealthy Street, S.E., Grand Rapids, Mich. 49506
Banner of Truth Trust
 78B Chiltern Street, London, W. 1, England
Bethany Fellowship
 6820 Auto Club Road, Minneapolis, Minn. 55431
Bethany Press
 Box 179, St. Louis, Mo. 63166
Bible Banner Press
 6125 Olson Highway, Minneapolis, Minn. 55422
Broadman Press
 127 Ninth Avenue, North, Nashville, Tenn. 37203
Broadman Supplies
 See Broadman Press

Catholic Library Association
 461 West Lancaster Avenue, Haverford, Penna. 19041

Christian Publications, Inc.
25 South Tenth Street, Harrisburg, Penna. 17101
Concordia Publishing House
3558 South Jefferson Avenue, St. Louis, Mo. 63118
Convention Press
127 Ninth Avenue, North, Nashville, Tenn. 37203

Wm. B. Eerdmans Publishing Co.
255 Jefferson Avenue, S.E., Grand Rapids, Mich. 49502

Forest Press, Inc.
Lake Placid Club, N.Y. 12946

Gospel Light Publications
725 Colorado, Glendale, Calif. 91205

Harper and Row, Publishers
49 East 33rd Street, New York, N.Y. 10016
Harrison Service
7415 Wayzata Blvd., Minneapolis, Minn. 55426

Inter-Varsity Press
Box 5, Downers Grove, Ill. 60515

John Knox Press
Box 1176, Richmond, Va. 23209
Judson Press
Valley Forge, Penna. 19481

Key Publishers
Box 991, Wheaton, Ill. 60187

Loizeaux Brothers, Inc.
Box 70, Neptune, N.J. 07753

The Macmillan Company
866 Third Avenue, New York, N.Y. 10022
Moody Press
820 North LaSalle Street, Chicago, Ill. 60610

Multnomah Press
8435 N.E. Glisan Street, Portland, Ore. 97220

National Geographic Society
17 and M Streets, N.W., Washington, D.C. 20036

Presbyterian & Reformed Publishing Co.
Box 185, Nutley, N.J. 07110

Fleming H. Revell Company
Old Tappan, N.J. 07675
Rutgers University Press
30 College Avenue, New Brunswick, N.J. 08903

Charles Scribner's Sons
597 Fifth Avenue, New York, N.Y. 10017
√**Scripture Press Publications**
1825 College Avenue, Wheaton, Ill. 60187
The Seabury Press, Inc.
815 Second Avenue, New York, N.Y. 10017
Harold Shaw
340 Gundersen Drive, Wheaton, Ill. 60187
The Shoe String Press, Inc.
955 Sherman. Avenue, Hamden, Conn. 06514
√ **Sword of the Lord Publishers**
Murfreesboro, Tenn. 37130

Tyndale House, Publishers
336 Gundersen Drive, Wheaton, Ill. 60187

University of Chicago Press
5750 Ellis Avenue, Chicago, Ill. 60637

The Westminster Press
Witherspoon Building, Philadelphia, Penna. 19107
H. W. Wilson Company
950 University Avenue, Bronx, N.Y. 10452

√ **Zondervan Publishing House**
1415 Lake Drive, S.E., Grand Rapids, Mich. 49506

Directory of Library Supply and Equipment Companies

Bro-Dart Industries
1609 Memorial Avenue, Williamsport, Penna. 17701

Demco Educational Corp.
Box 1488, Madison, Wis. 53701

Gaylord Bros., Inc.
P.O. Box 61, Syracuse, N.Y. 13201
and

Gaylord Bros., Inc.
P.O. Box 710, Stockton, Calif. 95201